摄影：陈云峰　　编撰：张　俊
Photographed by Chen Yunfeng Written by Zhang Jun

雲南古塔建築

Yunnan Ancient Pagodas

下册 Vol.2

云南出版集团公司
云南美术出版社
Yunnan Publishing Group Corporation
Yunnan Fine Arts Publishing House

云南古塔分布图

香格里拉
金沙江
石鼓
丽江
剑川
喜洲
大理
巍山
楚雄
昆明
乌蒙山
昭通
腾冲
保山
梁河
潞西
怒江
澜沧江
景东
红河
哀牢山
玉溪
江川
通海
弥勒
邱北
广南
石屏
建水
开远
文山
红河
临沧
普洱
景洪

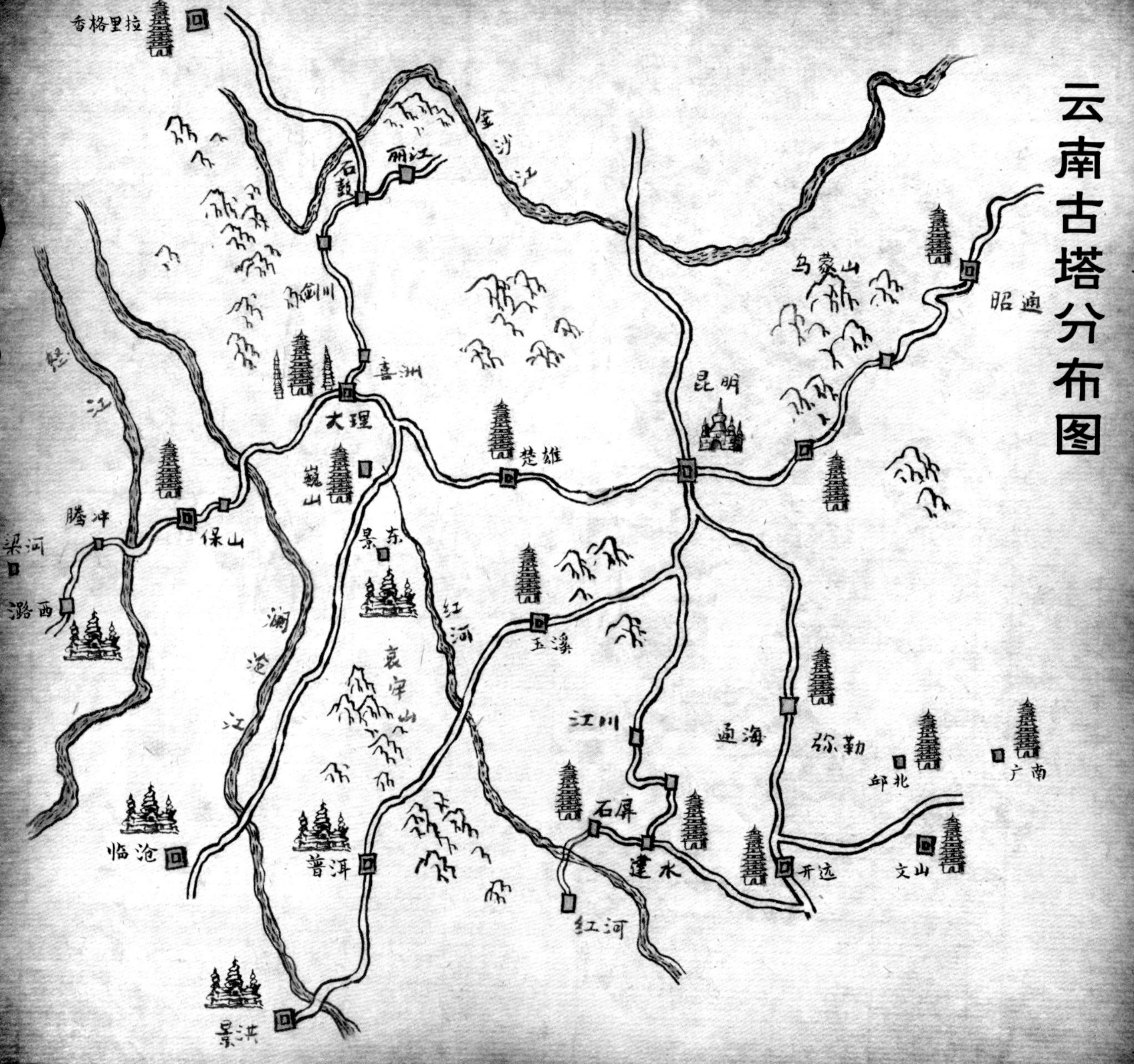

Contents

目录

临沧市

Lincang

勐旺塔　位于临沧市临翔区章驮乡勐旺村南约500米的山顶上。始建于明代。属南传上座部佛塔。台基为八角形，边长2.3米，高约2米，上砌八边“亚”字形须弥座，塔身分八面，为“串”字形塔身，似多层须弥座叠加而成。塔身一面设佛龛，为砖石结构实心塔，塔顶置石质葫芦状塔刹。通高约15米。每逢傣历新年赕塔者皆聚于塔下进行祭祀活动。为云南省文物保护单位。

Mengwang Pagoda is located on top of a hill about 500 meters south of Mengwang Village. The pagoda was built in the Ming Dynasty with an octagonal base about 2.3 m long on each side and 2 m tall. On the base is an octagonal X-shaped Sumeru seat with a gourd-shaped body. This 15-m tall pagoda is a totally solid pagoda and one side of the pagoda is designed with a shrine with a stone gourd-shaped kshetra on top of it. It is a provincial-grade cultural relic.

腊东塔　位于临沧市临翔区章驮乡腊东寨旁，原名“泰安塔”。始建年代不详，后多次修葺、重建。台基为八角形，边长2米，高约1.8米，开假门。砌“亚”字形须弥座，“串”字形塔身，正面下沿设佛龛。塔顶置葫芦状塔刹，标形刹尖。为砖石结构塔，通高约15米。

Ladong Pagoda is located near the Ladong Village, Zhangtuo, Linxiang, Liancang with an uncertain date of construction. It has since been restored and reconstructed. The base is in an octagonal shape about 2 meters on each side and some 1.8 m tall with a decorative gate. The top of the pagoda is a gourd-shaped spear point covered. The pagoda is constructed totally of bricks some 15 m in height.

临沧西塔　位于临沧市临翔区西2公里团山上，又称“白塔”、“西文笔塔”。始建于明天启元年（1621年），为傣族早期的佛塔。台基与塔身皆为八角形，“亚”字须弥座，砖石结构，“串”字形塔身，塔刹已残缺，通高约15米。为云南省文物保护单位。

Lincang West Pagoda is about two km west of Linxiang District, Lincang was built in the 1st year of the Tianqi Reign of the Ming Dynasty representing the earliest stūpa construction of the Dai ethnic group. This 15-m tall pagoda is placed on an octagonal and X-shaped Sumeru made up of bricks and stones. On top of the Sumeru seat is a gourd-shaped structure in company with an uncompleted kshetra. It is a provincial- important cultural relic under official protection.

景戈佛塔 位于临沧市耿马县城东南山顶景戈佛寺旁，又称大“白塔”。是临沧地区的第一大佛塔。始建于清乾隆四十三年（1778年）1988年大地震毁坏，后照原状重建。主塔高30米，须弥座由“亚”字形重叠构成，笋状塔身，塔身下部两级为多边形，每面开佛龛，上部为圆锥体。塔刹由塔针、铜伞、铜铃组成。须弥座和塔基的六个角各立小塔两座，高4米，饰有仰莲图案。赕塔期间，各族群众聚会白塔旁敬香、舞蹈。为耿马县文物保护单位。

Jingge Stūpa

It is located on top of the Nanshan Mountain east of Gengma Town seat, Lincang, and it was built in the 43rd year of the Qianlong Reign of the Qing Dynasty (About 1778). In 1988, it collapsed in an earthquake but it was later restored to its original state. This 30-m tall pagoda was built in an overlapped X-shape with a bamboo shoot body based on a 2-storey base. The base has shrines on each level. The kshetra is designed with stūpa pole, bronze umbrella, and bronze bells. On top of the Sumeru seat are 12 minor stūpas set on the six corners in pairs, and they are all four meters tall decorated with face-up lotus flowers and retained as a cultural relic under official protection.

沧源白塔　位于临沧市沧源县城郊约2公里，始建于清代，后多次修葺。塔高约12 米，塔的造型甚是独特，八角形台基，鼓形塔身，周围立8根方柱，上置葫芦宝顶。塔刹由粗壮的相轮、宝伞、银铃等组成。

Cangyuan White Pagoda

It is situated about 2 km off Cangyuan, Lincang built in the Qing Dynasty. It is placed on an octagonal base combined with a drum-shaped body surrounded with eight square columns to be finished with a treasure guard on top. The kshetra is composed of wheels, treasure umbrella and silver bells.

保山市
Baoshan

弄幕白塔　位于保山市隆阳区潞江坝新城村。始建年代不详，多次修葺。由主塔和24座小塔组成。方形台基，须弥座由“亚”字形重叠收缩构成，圆形仰莲台座，覆钟式塔身，塔刹修长，由多重相轮和宝伞(又称华盖)、银铃组成，主塔高16.5米。小塔为方形塔座，形制与大塔基本一致。须弥座正中各有一座佛龛。佛龛正脊、券门沿面有花草云纹装饰，雕刻精细，色彩艳丽，龛顶立小塔，如群星捧月环绕主塔。

Nongmu White Pagoda

It is located at Xincheng Village, Lujiangba, Longyang, Baoshan with an uncertain date of construction and it has been repaired several times in the past decades. The entire pagoda consists of a main pagoda and 24 baby pagodas all fixed on a square pedestal. The Sumeru seat was built in an X-shape and gradually closes up. The pagoda body was built in the shape of a round lotus seat and an overturned bell. The slim kshetra is composed of multi-wheels, treasure umbrella and silver bells. In total, the main pagoda is 16.5 m tall.

佛光寺塔　位于德宏州潞西市芒市镇佛光寺内。清道光十六年（1836年）兴建，后多次修葺。由主塔和16座小塔环绕组成。主塔高10.5米，“亚”字形须弥座，圆形仰莲台座，覆钟式塔身，塔刹较粗壮，由十一重相轮和宝伞、银铃等组成。小塔各高3.5米，下设方形券洞式佛龛，形制与主塔相似。须弥座和塔身上雕有莲瓣等彩色纹饰，主塔四角各立一尊彩色圆雕护法金刚像。为潞西市文物保护单位。

Foguang Monastery Pagoda

It is located inside the Foguang Monastery of Mangshi, Luxi, Dehong Autonomous Prefecture. It was built in the 16th year of Daoguang Reign of the Qing Dynasty (about 1836) and was repaired several times during its history. The 10.5-m tall main pagoda is surrounded by 16 baby pagodas all placed on an X-shaped Sumeru seat and supported by round lotus-shaped holders with an overturned-bell pagoda body in the middle. The strong kshetra is composed of 11-circled wheel and a treasure umbrella, as well as silver bells. The baby pagodas are all the same height up to 3.5 m tall with a square shrine each and they are all built in the same pattern as the main pagoda. In both the Sumeru seat and pagoda bodies are lotus petals engraved colorfully and vividly. Standing in four corners of the main pagoda are colored Dharmapala vajra statues. It is a cultural relic under Luxi official protection.

铁城佛塔　位于德宏州潞西市芒市镇团结大街南段，傣语称“广母姐列”，意为铁城佛塔，土司方作凡为纪念在战争的胜利而建。始建于清康熙年间，后多次修葺。为泰式金刚宝座实心砖塔，主塔高11.6米。八角形台基，边长2.15米。三层须弥座被菩提树根缠绕。塔刹由相轮、宝瓶、宝盖组成。台基四角各有小塔，三面设双坡顶式佛龛，门脊饰花鸟纹，有4只石雕“拉嘎”(傣族灵兽)守护。因塔中长出一棵30余米高的树，塔为树根包裹，故又称“树包塔”。为潞西市文物保护单位。

Tiecheng Pagoda-Stūpa

It is located in the south section of Tuanjie Avenue, Mangshi, Luxi, Dehong Prefecture. It was built to celebrate the victory in a local war. The pagoda was initially constructed during the Kangxi Reign of the Qing Dynasty and experienced several repairs in its history. It is a Thai-styled hard-core vajra pagoda made of bricks. The main pagoda is about 11.6 m tall placed on an octagonal base with a length of some 2.15 m on each side. It has three level Sumeru seats entangled with the roots of bodhidruma, thus, it is also called “Tree Wrapped Pagoda.” It is an officially protected cultural relic of Luxi Prefecture Government.

景罕佛塔 位于德宏州陇川县景罕镇东山坡，傣名“广母邦代”，为释迦牟尼转世的玉兔骨塔。始建于明天启三年（1623年），曾多次修葺、重建。主塔约高11米，须弥座台高宽大，上两层为折角“亚”字形，覆钵式塔身较小，塔刹由多重相轮、宝伞、银铃组成，特别粗壮。台基四面的小塔开双坡顶式佛龛，内供佛像。塔座洁白，塔身涂金粉。为德宏州文物保护单位。

Jinghan Pagoda-Stūpa

It is situated on the East Hillside of Jinghan, Longchuan, Dehong, built in the 3rd year of the Tianqi Reign of the Ming Dynasty (around 1623) and was repaired and reconstructed several times during its history. The main pagoda is about 11 m tall placed on a broad Sumeru seat dominated by an overturned-bowl pagoda body. The kshetra consists of multi-layer wheels, a treasure umbrella and silver bells, making it especially tough and strong. On the four sides of the pagoda are four baby pagodas built with shrines for holding Buddha statues. It is an officially protected relic of Luxi Prefecture Government.

风平佛塔　位于潞西市风平乡风平寨。始建于乾隆六年（1741年），曾两毁两建。四层“亚”字形退台须弥座，座顶饰仰莲，覆钟式塔身，塔刹较粗壮，由多重相轮、宝盖、铜铃组成，整体呈圆锥形，主塔高23米。四周环列28座小塔，各高7.5米，下设佛龛，形制与主塔相似。底座每方有一大佛龛，券门上装饰双龙，旁有石雕灵兽守护。逢傣族盛大节日，群众皆聚于塔下祭祀舞蹈。为潞西市文物保护单位。

Fengping Buddha-Stūpa

It is located in Fengping Village, Fengping, Luxi, Dehong and built in the 6th year of the Qianlong Reign of the Qing Dynasty (1741). Later, it was twice destroyed and restored. It has a four-layer X-shaped Sumeru seat holding a overturned-bell pagoda body. The kshetra is tough and strong with multi-wheels, a treasure cover, bronze bells, and shaped into a pyramid. The main pagoda is about 23 m tall surrounded with 28 baby pagodas all the same height up to 7.5 m evenly. The baby pagodas are all built with a shrine underneath and constructed in the same pattern as the main pagoda. It is an officially protected cultural relic of Luxi Municipal Government.

姐勒金塔　位于德宏州瑞丽市勐卯镇姐勒寨旁。建于清代，曾多次修葺、重建。传说此地夜间大放光芒，掘地发现佛骨，勐卯领主武定召建塔祀佛。为实心砖石结构，整体为圆锥体，“亚”字形须弥座。塔刹由十一重相轮组成，十分粗大，主塔高36米。16座小塔大小不一，环绕主塔，较大的塔底部设佛龛内供佛像，形制与主塔相似。为德宏州文物保护单位。

Jiele Golden Stūpa

It stands near Jiele Village, Mengmao, Ruili, Dehong and was built in the Qing Dynasty. It was repaired and reconstructed several times during its history. It is a solid-core brick pagoda in a pyramid placed on an X-shaped base. The kshetra is composed of 11-layer wheels to make it tough and strong. The main pagoda is about 36 m tall surrounded by 16 baby pagodas of uneven height. Some bigger pagodas are built with shrines. The Jiela Golden Pagoda is an official cultural relic reserve on the prefecture level.

弄安佛塔 位于瑞丽市城南1.3公里处。始建于清代，曾多次修葺，砖石结构。又称金鸭塔，傣语称“广母弄安”。传说古代一对金鸭带着傣家人找到了这片富饶美丽的地方，故在此建塔。主塔通高约15米，六角形须弥座，分三级，覆钟式塔身，金色塔刹，由多重相轮、宝伞、银铃组成。主塔旁有4座小塔。群塔塔身均有仰莲等浮雕装饰。第一层须弥座六面开设双坡顶式佛龛，内供佛像。为瑞丽市文物保护单位。

Nong'an Stūpa

It is located about 1.3 km south of Ruili built in the Qing Dynasty and it was repaired several times during its history. This 15-m tall brick-made pagoda is placed on a hexagonal Sumeru seat graded into six layers. On top of the sumeru is an overturn-bell pagoda body combined with multi-circle wheels, a treasure umbrella and silver bells. Surrounding the main pagoda are four baby pagodas finished in the same manner as the main pagoda with lotus and significant relief work. The first layer was built with six double-eave shrines. It is a cultural relic reserve at the Ruili Municipal level.

允燕塔　位于德宏州盈江县平原镇允燕村，又称“孟町塔”。始建于1947年。为镇水祈丰而建。群塔由1座主塔和44座小塔组成。塔通高24.9米，台基占地400余平方米，须弥座为折角“亚”字形，分3层，覆钟式塔身，塔刹粗壮，由多重相轮、铜质宝伞、风铎银铃组成。塔座为洁白的圆形仰莲台，饰多种几何形图案，涂金粉。台基前有石雕“拉嘎”(傣族灵兽)守护。小塔如众星捧月，拱卫四周，净高约4米，下开方形券洞式佛龛，内供佛像，形制与主塔相似。允燕塔是云南最大的南传上座部群塔。为全国重点文物保护单位。

Yunyan Pagoda

It is located in Yunyan Village, Pingyuan, Yingjiang, Dehong and built in 1947. The entire pagoda cluster consists of one main pagoda and 44 baby pagodas. The main pagoda is about 24.9 m tall occupying some 400 square meters. All pagodas are all placed on an X-shaped Sumeru seat graded into three layers. The overturned-bell pagoda body was built with tough and strong kshetra composed of multi-circle wheels, a bronze treasure umbrella and silver bells. The pagoda seat is a pure white round pedestal engraved with a face-up lotus flower integrated with ornamental patterns coated with golden color. In front of the pedestal stands a stone-carved *Laga*, a spiritual beast *Laga* adored by the local Dai people, which is a guard of the pagoda. The height of baby pagodas is 4m tall evenly built with shrines. It is considered the most important Southern Buddhist pagoda in Yunnan. It is a nationally-important cultural relic.

梁河白塔　位于德宏州梁河县城内。始建于清代，为泰式金刚宝座空心砖塔。由主塔和4座小塔组成。主塔约高14米，八角形须弥座，塔身由折角“亚”字形须弥座和覆钟形组成，塔刹由相轮、银铃等组成。小塔底部各开一塔门，大小塔身饰有几何花纹、浮雕图案。塔座四周设围栏。

Lianghe White Pagoda

It is situated in Lianghe, Dehong and it was initially built in the Qing Dynasty. This Thai-styled hollow-core brick vajra-pagoda is about 14 m tall with a main pagoda and four baby pagodas all fixed on an octagonal Sumeru seat. The pagoda body consists of an X-shaped Sumeru seat and an overturn-bell structure, together with kshetra, wheels, and silver bells. The lower parts of the baby pagodas are built with arches.

普洱市
Pu'er

芒蚌佛塔 位于普洱市思茅港镇芒蚌村东。始建于清代。方形台基，高0.9米，饰有浮雕图案。塔身为三层鼓形重叠而成，高4.5米。塔刹为石质葫芦宝顶。台基稍有损坏，全塔保存完好。为普洱市思茅区文物保护单位。

Mangbeng Buddha-Stūpa

It was built in the Qing Dynasty and is now located in the east of Mangbeng Village, Simaogang, Pu'er. The stūpa is placed on a 0.9 m high base decorated with relief. The stūpa's body consists of 3-layer drum shapes overlapped up to 4.5 m in height . The kshetra is made of stone with a treasure guard top. Except for some parts of the base which are damaged, the stūpa remains in good condition. It is a culture relic of the Simao area.

孟连大金塔　　位于普洱市孟连县娜允镇南垒河畔。始建年代不详，后曾多次修葺、重建。群塔建在圆形的塔座上，由主塔和16座小塔组成。主塔通高31米，下部为“串”字形，上部为覆钟式。塔刹由多重相轮、宝伞、银铃组成。小塔下开双坡顶式佛龛，顶上有更最小的塔。须弥座和龛顶为白色，所有塔身均为金色。由于汉文化与傣文化的融合，佛龛内供有汉传佛教的弥勒佛，地宫里绘有《西游记》壁画等。

Menglian Grand Golden Pagoda

With an uncertain date of construction, the Grand Golden Pagoda in Menglian, repaired and reconstructed several times in the past, is now located by the Nanlei River, Nayun, Menglian, Pu'er. It is composed of one main pagoda and 16 baby pagodas. The main golden pagoda is about 31 m tall with a shrine built in the lower part and the smallest pagoda on top. The amalgamation of mainland culture and Thai culture is remarkably represented in the frescos of Journey to the West in the basement palace.

上城佛寺塔　位于孟连县娜允镇上城佛寺内。佛寺原为土司家族专用，始建于清同治年间(1868年)。由两座形制大同小异的佛塔和两座亭阁式小塔组成，台阶上的佛塔一座约高11米，另一座略矮，皆为方形折角"亚"字形须弥座，塔身为覆钟式，塔刹由多重相轮、宝伞、银铃组成。两座亭阁式小塔各分两级，每级皆开佛龛，为"亚"字形须弥座，通高3.6米。

Shangcheng Buddha Temple Pagoda

Within the Buddha Temple at Shangcheng, Nayun, Menglian is a pagoda which used to be a special place reserved for the chieftain family, and it was initially built during the Tongzhi Reign of the Qing Dynasty (1868). It consists of two quite similar Buddha-stūpas together with two small pavilion pagodas in the front. The Buddha-stūpas on top of the pedestal are almost 11 m tall each and both are fixed to an X-shaped Sumeru seat. Over the overturned-bell body is a kshetra composed of multi-wheels, a treasure umbrella and silver bells. The other two pavilion styled pagodas (3.6 m) have two grades opened with shrines on each grade.

芒洪八角塔 位于普洱市澜沧县惠民乡芒洪寨，始建于清代，为八角形重檐攒尖顶空心砖塔，通高5.8米，塔基为砂石，八边形须弥座，高1.6米，塔身高2.1米，直径3.36米。底层西方设塔门，另外七方嵌石雕图案。塔刹为八角攒尖顶，檐下绘有古代兵器，塔身内藏经书。1985年公布为县级文物保护单位。

Manghong Octagonal Pagoda

It is situated in Manghong Village, Huimin, Lancang, Pu'er, and it was built in the Qing Dynasty. This pagoda is made up of brick about 5.8 m tall fixed in a sandstone foundation. The octagonal Sumeru seat is about 1.6 m high and the pagoda body is 2.1 m in height and 3.36 m in diameter. The pagoda entrance is open in the west of the bottom layer on one side and the remaining seven sides are embedded with carved drawings. The kshetra is formed into an octagonal point painted with ancient arms below the eave. Inside the pagoda body are sutra scrolls kept secretly. In 1985, it was listed as one of the county relics.

下允佛塔　位于普洱市澜沧县上允镇下允寨下允佛寺旁。始建于清咸丰年间（1860年），曾多次修葺。塔座为方形“亚”字形须弥座，塔身呈串字形，饰有仰莲浮雕，塔刹为莲座上插金属刹杆，通高约6.5米。须弥座四角各立小塔，高0.9米，形制与主塔相同，无塔刹。为澜沧县文物保护单位。

Xiayun Buddha-Stūpa

It is situated by the Xiayun Buddha Temple, Xiayun Village, Shangyun, Lancang, Pu'er, built in the Xianfeng Reign of the Qing Dynasty and repaired several times in the past. The pagoda has a square Sumeru seat in the shape of an "x", and the pagoda body was built into a gourd-shape decorated with a face-up lotus. The kshetra is a kind of metal pole inserted into a lotus seat up to 6.5 meters in height. On the four corners of the Sumeru seat are four baby pagodas about 0.9 m tall each without kshetras. It is a cultural relic under official protection locally.

整董贺塔 位于普洱市江城县整董镇曼贺井村小山顶上。始建于清道光年间，由整董土司召承恩所建，民国十七年(1928年)重修。从台基至须弥座均为方形，方形覆钟式塔身，通高7.5米，塔顶为圆形花瓶，塔刹由刹杆、宝伞、银铃组成。在傣族佛塔中未发现与此形状相同者。为江城县文物保护单位。

Zhengdonghe Pagoda

It is located on top of a small hill near Manhejing Village, Zhengdong, Jiangcheng, Pu'er, built in the Daoguang Ear of the Qing Dynasty, and reconstructed in 1928. The pagoda was built completely in a square shape from the pedestal to semeru base including an overturned-bell pagoda body. The pagoda is about 7.5 m tall with a round flower vase on top, while the kshetra consists of a pole, an umbrella and silver bells. It is a cultural relic under the official protection in Jiangcheng County.

景宰塔　位于江城县整董镇曼乱宰寨。始建时间不明，后多次修葺、重修。主塔通高6.7米，“亚”字形须弥座，覆钟式塔身，塔刹由多重相轮、宝伞组成。须弥座四角各立小塔，高3.6米，主塔下开佛龛，小塔下开券洞式佛龛，形制与主塔相同。有五台石阶通须弥座，两旁塑“拉嘎”(傣族灵兽)守护。

Jingzai Pagoda

It stands in the Manluanzai Village, Zhengdong, Jiancgheng with an uncertain date of construction, and it was repaired and reconstructed several times during its history. The main pagoda is about 6.7 m tall fixed to an X-shaped Sumeru seat with an overturned-bell pagoda body on top. The kshetra is composed of multi-wheels and a treasure umbrella. On the semeru base are four baby pagodas about 3.6 m tall each erected on the corners with shrines built in the lower parts. Both the main pagoda and the baby pagodas are built in the same form connected with a five-step staircase leading to the Sumeru seat in company with a stone carved animal called '*Laga*,' as a guard of the pagoda.

曼贺塔　位于江城县整董曼贺寨。始建年代不详，曾多次修葺、重修。村民建塔为祈风调雨顺粮食丰收，故又称丰收塔。须弥座为六角形，塔身为"串"字形六面体，下面六面开佛龛，旁有浮雕石龙一对，顶部为宝珠葫芦顶，塔刹由相轮、宝伞等组成。塔通高约11米，为砖石结构的实心塔。

Manhe Pagoda

It is situated in Manhe Village, Zhengdong, Jiangcheng with an uncertain date of construction remains in good condition through several repairs and reconstruction during its history. The pagoda body is about 11 m tall built into a hexahedron gourd-shape with six shrines in the lower parts associated with a pair of stone carved dragon nearby. On top of the pagoda is embedded a precious-pearl guard and the kshetra is composed of wheels, and a treasure umbrella.

勐卧双塔　位于普洱市景谷县威远镇大寨勐卧佛寺。由威远土官刀汉臣建于明末，道光十八年（1838年）修葺。两座塔形制相似，砖石结构，方形台基，须弥座为“亚”字形多层重叠，塔身为砖砌覆钟式，两塔相距30米。两座塔身都先后长出榕树，塔与树交织为一体，树高出塔身近20米，塔刹均被树所替代。右塔为“塔包树”，高7.2米，左塔为“树包塔”，高10.7米。清道光《威远厅志》曾载：“塔中生缅树，其枝从石缝内周围伸出，枝叶甚茂，塔石不崩……名曰塔树”　双塔的台基与须弥座上刻有《唐僧取经》等佛经故事，体现了傣汉文化的交融，还有民间传说《孔雀公主》和动植物浮雕图案，两旁有石雕狮子。为云南省文物保护单位。

Mengwo Twin Pagodas

Found inside the Mengwo Buddha Temple are two pagodas similarly built not far from Dazhai, Weiyuan, Jinggu, Pu'er. As it is recorded the twin pagodas were officially built at the end of the Ming Dynasty by an aboriginal official named Dao Hanchen and repaired in the 18th year of Daoguang Reign in the Qing Dynasty (1838). These twin pagodas are both made of bricks supported with square pedestals connected with overlapped X-shaped sumeru seats pointing upward. The pagodas' bodies are made into overturned-bells set apart with a distance of some 30 meters. What makes the twin pagodas extraordinarily important is that they both coexist with banyan trees interlinked into one body, thus, the kshetras are both replaced by the tree branches. Only the left pagoda is wrapped by banyan tree while the right pagoda contains the banyan tree growing from inside outward. On the pedestals of these two pagodas (10.7 m) are written the story of an ancient Chinese monk who travelled a long distance to the west in order to learn the true Buddhism sutra. As a matter of the fact, it is a living record telling the descendents about the cultural blending of the Han people with the Dai locals. Additionally, some local legends and plants are also engraved in company with a pair of stone lions standing by. It is a provincial-grade cultural relic under official protection.

曼崩铜塔　　傣语名“塔瑞董”，意为山坡上的铜塔。位于西双版纳州勐腊县勐腊镇曼崩寨旁。清代由塔木密拉建造，1759年重修时用铜皮包裹塔身，上世纪中铜皮已全部锈蚀损坏。台基为方形“亚”字须弥座，塔身呈串字形，从下而上逐层收分，塔刹由相轮、银铃等组成。台基上设佛龛，四周设围栏，上雕卧龙，门两侧立石象。为勐腊县文物保护单位。

Manbeng Bronze Pagoda

In the Dai language, it is called Ta Rui Dong, meaning the bronze pagoda on the hillside. It is located by the Manbeng Village, Mengla, Xishuangbanna and was built in the Qing Dynasty by Tamumila. Later on, it was rebuilt into a bronze coated body in 1759. The square pedestal was built into an X-shaped sumeru seat on top of which is a gourd-shaped pagoda body gradually dwindling upward. The kshetra is made up of wheels and silver bells. It is a cultural relic of Mengla County under official protection.

曼竜勒金塔 位于勐腊县勐伴镇曼竜勒寨旁的山上。始建于清代，后多次修葺。全塔为金色，方形台基，折角“亚”字形高须弥座，六角形须弥座式塔身，覆钟式塔顶，塔刹由多重相轮、宝伞、银铃组成，通高约13米。须弥座下部四方设双坡顶式佛龛，台基四周设围栏，旁边建亭阁式大佛龛，内供一组佛像。

Manlongle Golden Pagoda

On top of the mountain by the Manlongle Village, Manban, Mengla stands a golden pagoda named right after the village with an uncertain date of construction experienced several repairs in the history. The pagoda (13 m tall) is built on a square pedestal overlapped by a folded-edge X-shaped sumeru seat. In addition, the entire body is formed into hexagonal sumeru connecting to an overturned bell top and a kshetra composed of wheels, treasure umbrella and silver bells. In the lower part of the sumeru seat are double-sloped shrines in the four sides in company with a large shrine nearby, in which a pair of Buddha statues are placed.

曼暖叫佛塔

位于勐腊县勐腊镇曼暖叫寨。始建于清代，后多次修葺。群塔为金色，方形台基，主塔通高约15米，塔身为折角“亚”字形须弥座重叠组成，覆钟式塔顶，塔刹由多重相轮、宝伞、银铃组成。四座小塔建在台基4角，高约9米，形制与主塔相似。须弥座四面开佛龛。群塔周设围栏，上雕卧龙。

Mangnuanjiao Stūpa

Built in the Qing Dynasty and repaired several times during its history, the pagoda is found at Mangnuanjiao Village, Mengla. The entire pagoda is about 15 meters tall situated on a square pedestal connected to a folded-edge sumeru seat in an X-shape overlapped with an overturned-bell summit. The kshetra consists of multi-layer wheels, treasure umbrella and silver bells. The four small pagodas set on the corners are some 9 m evenly all in the same pattern as the main pagoda. On the four sides of the sumeru seat are shrines. The pagoda group is protected by surrounding guardrails engraved with dragons.

曼降佛塔　位于勐腊县勐腊镇曼降寨。始建年代不详，后多次修葺。由土塔和小塔组成群塔，方形台基，主塔通高约12米，塔身为方形重叠折角“亚”字形须弥座，覆钟式塔顶，塔刹由圆形仰莲与相轮、宝伞、银铃组成。双重须弥座，四角各立4座小塔，与主塔融为一体，座下设佛龛，形制与主塔约有不同。

Manjiang Stūpa

The pagoda is located in Manjiang Village, Mengla with an unclear date of construction and known to have been repaired several times during its history. The main pagoda is about 12 m tall surrounded by four baby pagodas all situated in a square pedestal built into an X-shape. On top of the pedestal is an overturned-bell pagoda summit while the kshetra is composed of a round face-up lotus flower, wheels, a treasure umbrella and silver bells. On top of the double layer sumeru seat are four baby pagodas differently built from the main pagoda but they are connected with the main pagoda into one group built with shrines in the bottom layers.

波龙塔　　位于勐腊县勐棒镇。始建于清代，后多次修葺。方形台基，八角锥体须弥座，塔身为八角多层须弥座叠加的“串”字形，上部为两层圆形仰莲台，塔刹由相轮、银铃等组成，主塔通高14.5米。须弥座下开双坡顶式佛龛。台基四角立4座小塔，通高8.3米，造型与主塔相似。台基建于石阶上，石级两侧有雕塑卧龙盘桓，后为孔雀开屏浮雕。

Bolong Pagoda

Built in the Qing Dynasty but known to have been repaired several times during its history, the pagoda is located presently in Mengbang, Mengla. This 14.5m tall pagoda was built on a square pedestal connected to an octagonal sumeru seat. The body of the pagoda is an overlapped gourd-shaped octagonal sumeru seat with shrines in the lower part, on top of which are two layers of face-up lotus flower platforms. The kshetra consists of wheels and silver bells. In the corners of the pedestal are four baby pagodas about 8.3 m evenly built in the same pattern as the main pagoda.

曼梭醒佛塔　位于勐腊县勐仑镇曼梭醒寨罗梭江右岸。又名塔庄董，始建于清代，后多次修葺。台基约两米高，石阶作通道，台基四角各置石雕“拉嘎”(灵兽)守护。须弥座、塔身皆为八角锥形，三层须弥座叠砌为“串”字形，上为覆钟式塔身，塔刹由相轮、银铃、多重宝伞组成。塔通高12.8米。

Mansuoxing Stūpa

On the right bank of the Luosuo River by Mansuoxing Village, Menglun, Mengla stands the Mansuoxing Stūpa (12.8 m) built in the Qing Dynasty and repaired several times. The 2-m pedestal was built with a stone staircase and stone carved '*Laga*' (a kind worshipped spiritual animal) on the four corners. The pedestal, the sumeru seat and the pagoda body are all octagonal shapes. On top of the three-layer sumeru seat is a gourd-shape covered with an overturned bell body. The kshetra consists of wheels, silver bells, and multi-layer treasure umbrellas.

曼岗纳金塔　位于勐腊县勐腊镇曼岗纳寨。始建于清代，后多次修葺。群塔由主塔和10座小塔环绕组成。方形台基，五层折角“亚”字形须弥座，四面开双坡顶式佛龛。塔身由“串”字形叠加覆钟式组成。塔刹由多重相轮、宝伞、银铃组成。整体呈圆锥体，通高约19米。10座小塔大小不一，分立在台基和须弥座上。台基上塑5尊头顶宝伞的坐姿佛像，每尊高0.8米。佛像与群塔皆为金色，围院护墙塑有8条彩色卧龙。

Mangang'na Golden Pagoda

Built in the Qing Dynasty, the Mangang'na Golden Pagoda, at Mangang'na Village, Mengla, Jinghong, has experienced several repairs. The main pagoda (19m) is in company with 10 baby surrounding pagodas, all fixed on a square pedestal, and continuously connected to a five-layer X-shaped sumeru seat with shrines built in four sides. The gourd-shaped body connects to an overturned-bell, on top of which is the kshetra composed of wheels, treasure umbrella and silver bells. The entire pagoda takes the shape of a taper towering up some 19 meters. The 10 baby pagodas distributed on the pedestal and sumeru seat are built in different sizes and scales. Additionally, there are five sitting Buddhas' statues with treasure umbrellas molded on the pedestal about 0.8 meters tall each.

城子塔　　位于勐腊县勐仑镇城子寨北。始建于清代，后多次修葺。群塔由主塔和4座小塔组成。主塔为六角形须弥座，边长1.7米。塔身呈圆锥形，塔刹由圆形仰莲台与相轮、宝伞、银铃组成，通高13.4 米。方形台基四角立4座小塔，高4.5米。台基的石阶旁立一对石雕“拉嘎”（灵兽）守护。群塔为金色。

Chengzi Pagoda

Built in the Qing Dynasty and repaired several times during its history, the Chengzi Pagoda is now located north of Chengzi Village in Menglun, Mengla. This is a group of golden pagodas composed of one main pagoda and four baby pagodas all fixed in a hexagonal sumeru seat about 1.7m each side in length. The pagoda body takes the shape of a taper attached to a round kshetra that is composed of wheels, treasure umbrella and silver bells, making the entire height some 13.4 m. On top of the square pedestal are four baby pagodas about 4.5 m each, with a pair of stone carved *Laga* standing by the stairs.

召庄发塔　位于景洪市勐罕镇景宽寨旁的小山上。始建于清代中期，后多次修葺。为金刚宝座式塔。方形台基上由主塔和4座小塔组成群塔。主塔另起八角形台基，折角“亚”字形须弥座，塔身由“串”字形加覆钟组成，塔刹由多重相轮、宝伞、银铃组成，通高16米。小塔下方开佛龛，形制与主塔相似。台基四周饰有仰莲图案，四面石阶旁立“拉嘎”（灵兽）和卧龙。全塔为金色。

Zhaozhuang Prosperity Pagoda

On top of the hill near JIngkuan Village in Menghan, Jinghong is a group of golden pagodas, also vajra-pagoda, named as Prosperity Pagoda built in the Qing Dynasty and repaired several times during its history. On top of the square pedestal are the main pagoda and four baby pagodas forming a large pagoda group. Additionally, the main pagoda (16 m) is exclusively built on an octagonal pedestal with a folded-edge X-shaped sumeru seat, whose body was built into a gourd-shape plus an overturned-bell. The kshetra consists of multi-layer wheels, a treasure umbrella and silver bells. In the lower parts of the baby pagodas are built shrines all in the same pattern as the main pagoda. Around the pedestal are decorations with face-up lotus flowers associated with *Laga* and dragons guarding closeby.

召庄密塔　位于景洪市勐罕镇澜沧江渡口旁的佛寺内。始建于清初，后多次修葺与重建。形制为金刚宝座塔，方形台基上由主塔和4座小塔组成群塔。主塔下另加筑六角形台基，折边“亚”字形重叠须弥座，覆钟式塔身，塔刹由圆形仰莲、相轮、宝伞、银铃组成，通高12米。小塔下方开佛龛，台基四周饰圆雕仰莲，台基旁设供品座，石阶旁立一对石雕“拉嘎”（灵兽）。全塔为金色。

Zhaozhuang mi Pagoda

Within the monastery by the pier of Lancang River near Manghan, Jinghong is the Zhaozhuangmi Pagoda built in the beginning of the Qing Dynasty experienced several repairs throughout the history. This golden pagoda group takes up the pattern of vajra-pagoda placed on a square pedestal consisting of one main pagoda (12 m) and four baby pagodas. Under the main pagoda are an additional hexagonal pedestal with foled-edge X-shaped sumeru seat. On top of the pedestal is the pagoda body in an overturned-bell shape. Upward is the kshetra composed of face-up lotus flower, wheels, treasure umbrella and silver bells. In the lower parts of the baby pagodas are shrines, and the pedestals are decorated with round lotus flower in carving. By the pagoda base is an offerings table safeguarded by a pair of stone carved Lagas.

曼春满佛寺塔 位于景洪市勐罕镇曼春满公园西南。佛寺与佛塔始建于清乾隆六年（1741年），后多次修葺与重建。形制为泰式金刚宝座式塔，由主塔和4座小塔组成群塔。主塔通高约12米，折角“亚”字形须弥座叠加覆钟式塔身，塔刹由圆形仰莲台、相轮、宝伞、银铃组成。小塔下开双坡顶式佛龛。台基四方立石雕“拉嘎”（灵兽）。群塔为金色。为云南省文物保护单位。

Manchunman Temple Pagoda

In the southwest of Manchunman Park, Menghan, Jinghong is the golden pagoda located built in the 6th year of the Qianlong Reign of the Qing Dynasty (1741), and it remains in good condition being repairs and reconstructed several times in the history. It is typical Thai styled vajra-pagoda composed of one main pagoda (12 m) and four baby pagodas all placed in an X-shaped sumeru seat overlapped by an overturned-bell pagoda body. The kshetra consists of face-up lotus flower, wheels, treasure umbrella and silver bells. In the lower parts of the baby pagodas are double-slope eave shrines and the pedestal is safeguarded on the four sides by stone carved Laga*s* as well.

曼听树包塔 位于景洪市勐罕镇曼听寨内。始建年代不详，后多次修葺。群塔由组塔和4座小塔组成。主塔仅存六角“亚”字形须弥座两层，须弥座上长出一棵10余米高的菩提树，树根缠绕塔身，塔身与塔刹已被树所代替，故有“树包塔”之称。4座小塔分两对，每对形制不同，台基座、塔身、塔刹一应俱全，保存完好，约高2.5米，基座与塔身有花纹与几何形浮雕图案装饰。

Manting Tree Wrapped Pagoda

This is a group of golden pagodas consisting of one main pagoda and four baby pagodas withan uncertain date of construction in the Manting Village near Menghan Town, Jinghong. The main pagoda is now only two layers of sumeru seat remained in hexagonal shape with a ten-meter high Bodhidhuma growing from inside the pagoda. The tree roots and branches enwinding the pagoda making them into one body and the kshetra has been replaced all by the branches outgoing, thus the local people call it Tree Embraced Pagoda as nickname. The four baby pagodas are divided into two parts and two for each only built differently. The four baby pagodas (2.5 m each) are all remaining in good conditions including the pedestal, the bodies, and the kshetras. Both the pedestal and pagoda body are decorated with flowers and clusters of reliefs.

曼听白塔　位于景洪市勐罕镇曼听佛寺内。始建年代不详，后多次修葺与重建。群塔由主塔和4座小塔组成。主塔的须弥座与塔身皆为八角锥形，塔身由须弥座叠砌为“串”字形与覆钟组成，塔刹由相轮、银铃、宝伞组成，通高约13米。小塔形制与主塔相同。阶梯式台基四周饰有彩绘、圆雕仰莲，四角置双坡顶式佛龛。现塔为近年重建。

Manting White Pagoda

Within the Buddha Temple in Manting, Menghan, Jinghong is the White Pagoda without a clear date of construction and repaired several times during its history. The group of pagodas is made up of one main pagoda (13 m) and four baby pagodas all placed on an octagonal sumeru seat. The body of the pagoda was built into an octagonal taper connected to a gourd-shaped sumeru seat and an overturned-bell structure. The kshetra is composed of wheel, silver bells and treasure umbrella. All the baby pagodas are built in the same pattern as the main one. The graded pedestal is engraved with colorful paintings, altorelievo of face-up lotus flowers, together with double cover shrines built only recently.

景哈金塔 位于景洪市景哈乡景哈村。约建于清代，后多次修葺与重建。为金刚宝座塔，由主塔和4座小塔组成。主塔为折角“亚”字形须弥座，塔身由八角形“串”字形加覆钟式组成，塔刹由多重相轮、宝伞、银铃组成，通高约14米。小塔下设佛龛，方形台基四周饰有浮雕仰莲，四面有石阶通达，有双龙护栏。群塔为金色。

Manha Golden Pagoda

In the Manha Village, Manha, Jinghong is a golden pagoda named after the village built approximately in the Qing Dynasty. It is a vajra pagoda experienced several repairs and reconstructions in the history. This is a group of golden vajra-pagoda made up of one main pagoda (14 m) and four baby pagodas placed on a folded-edge X-shaped sumeru seat. The pagoda body was built in an octagonal shape combined with an overturned-bell top. The kshetra is composed of multi-layer wheels, a treasure umbrella and silver bells. In the lower parts are shrines built in association with reliefs, guardrails and stone carved dragons around the pedestal.

景先塔　位于景洪市勐罕镇曼法村。始建于清初，后多次修葺与重建。群塔由主塔和8座小塔组成。台基为不规则圆形，折角“亚”字形须弥座，“串”字形塔身，塔刹由多重相轮、银铃等组成，通高约16米。须弥座与塔身开佛龛，全塔为金色。台基四面立雕塑“拉嘎”（灵兽）。

Manxian Pagoda

Built in the early Qing Dynasty and repaired several times during its history, this is a group of golden pagodas made up of one main pagoda (16 m) and eight baby pagodas fixed to an irregular round pedestal with a folded-edge X-shaped sumeru seat and a gourd-shaped body. Over the body is the kshetra composed of multi-layer wheels and silver bells. Both the sumeru seats and the pagoda body are built with shrines. On the four sides of the pedestal are statues of Iaga guarding the pagoda group.

曼景勐塔　位于景洪市勐龙镇曼景勐寨佛寺内，寺与塔始建于清代，后多次修葺。塔基为圆形，高0.6米。须弥座为圆形束腰，塔身为覆钟式，周边饰仰莲。塔刹由仰莲、相轮、宝伞、银铃组成。通高11.4米。塔基四角各立柱形圆雕仰莲，开小佛龛。

Manjingmeng Pagoda

Inside the Buddha Temple of Manjingmeng Village, Menglong, Jinghong is a pagoda built in the Qing Dynasty at the same time as the temple. Over its long history, the pagoda (11.4m tall) has been repeatedly repaired to keep it in good condition. It has a round pedestal about 0.6m high from the ground with a drum-styled sumeru seat shrunk in half-way. The overturned-bell body of the pagoda is decorated with face-up lotus flowers with a kshetra on top composed of wheels, treasure umbrella and silver bells. One the four sides of the pedestal corners are erected round columns engraved with face-up lotus flowers and small shrines.

景旺塔　位于景洪市勐龙镇曼龙扣村。始建年代不详，后多次修葺与重建。为泰式金刚宝座塔，由主塔和4座小塔组成。六角形台基饰有三层簇花、香草纹装饰。四边形花瓣须弥座的四角各开双坡顶式佛龛。主塔为圆形宝珠“串”字形塔身，塔刹由圆形仰莲台与相轮、宝伞、银铃组成，通高约12米。小塔分立佛龛顶，簇拥主塔，形制与主塔相同。群塔为金色。

Jingwang Pagoda

With an uncertain date of construction, the pagoda is found in Manglongkou Village, Menglong, Jinghong repaired and reconstructed several times during its history. It is a Thai-styled vajra-pagoda, completely covered in gold color and made up of one main pagoda and four baby pagodas all placed on a hexagonal pedestal decorated with three layers of flowers and fragrant plants around about. The flower-shaped quadrilateral sumeru seat has double sloped shrines in four corners. The main pagoda is altogether 12 m tall built into a round gourd-shaped precious pearl. The kshetra is composed of a face-up lotus pedestal, wheels, a treasure umbrella and silver bells. Each small pagoda has an individual shrine in the same pattern as the main pagoda.

曼飞龙塔　位于景洪市勐龙镇曼飞龙寨的后山上。始建于南宋（1203年），后多次修葺与重建。相传正南佛龛下的岩石上有释迦牟尼的足印。傣名“塔糯庄龙”，意为极大的笋塔。群塔为泰式金刚宝座塔，由主塔和9座小塔组成。须弥座为圆形，主塔塔身呈圆锥形，塔刹由圆形仰莲台与相轮、宝伞、银铃组成，通高16.29米。小塔形制与主塔相似，通高8.3米。群塔皆为白色。

台基周围设8个双坡顶式佛龛，龛内各供佛像一尊，龛壁上有许多浮雕佛像，形成众佛齐聚的图景。佛龛正脊、券门上有花草云纹装饰，雕刻精细，色彩艳丽，金碧辉煌，是傣族民间工艺的精华。为全国重点文物保护单位。

Manfeilong Pagoda

It is situated on the hilltop behind the Manfeilong Village, Menglong, Jinghong built initially in the South Song Dynasty (1203). It has been repaired and reconstructed several times in its history. It is said in local legends that a piece of rock under the shrine was engraved with the footprints of Sakyamuni. The entire pagoda group is pure while built into the Thai-styled vajra-pagoda composed of one main pagoda (16.29 m) and nine baby pagodas (8.3 m) all fixed to a round sumeru seat. The body of the main pagoda was built into a dome shape with a kshetra on top, which consists of wheels, a treasure umbrella and silver bells.

Around the pedestal are eight double sloped shrines holding a Buddha statue each. The wall of each shrine is engraved with little Buddha reliefs to highlight the shrine with the gathering of Buddhas. Along the central spines and arch edge of the shrines are exquisite decorations of flowers, grass and clouds. This pagoda group tops the list of protected national cultural relics.

曼纳囡塔　位于景洪市勐龙镇曼坡寨旁的山上。始建年代不详，后多次修葺与重建。群塔由主塔和4座小塔组成，方形台基，须弥座与塔身由折边“亚”字形重叠组成，上下收分显著。塔刹由宝珠、相轮、宝伞、银铃组成。主塔通高19.6米。小塔立于四角，较矮小，开佛龛。台基四周无围栏，四面有亭阁式塔门，四角设亭阁式佛龛座。西面为主塔门，两侧塑洗发的土地神“妥纳妮”。

Manna Baby Pagoda

Located on a hilltop of Manpo Village Menglong, Jinghong with an uncertain date of construction, the pagoda was repaired several times during its history. The pagoda group consists of one main pagoda and four small pagodas all fixed on a square pedestal connected with a sumeru seat finished remarkably at the edge in an overlapped X-shape. The kshetra is composed of precious pearls, wheels, a treasure umbrella and silver bells. The main pagoda is about 19.6 m tall with the four small pagodas standing on the corners lower in height and built with shrines. On the four sides of the pedestal are also pavilion-styled gates and four pavilion-styled shrines.

帕雅天叫甲山墓塔

位于景洪市勐龙镇曼景列村旁。始建于民国初年，后多次修葺。帕雅天叫甲山是清末勐龙地区的著名佛爷，至今当地和东南亚的信众常来祭拜。塔基、塔台、须弥座皆为圆形，覆钟式塔身，塔刹由，仰莲台、相轮、宝伞、银铃组成，通高6.2米。台基四方立双坡顶式佛龛。全塔为金色，用几何浮雕图案和彩绘装饰。

Payatian Jiaojiashan Stūpa is situated on the side of Manlie Village in Menglong, Jinghong. It was built during the 1910s and has been renovated several times afterwards. The pagoda is so named after famous Buddha named Payatian Jiaojiashan during the Menglong Reign of the Qing Dynasty. It is a golden colored stūpa of about 6.2m tall with an overturned bell-shaped body on a circular pedestal and Sumeru seat decorated with relief and colorful ornaments. The kshetra is placed on an upturned lotus pedestal with wheels, an ornamental parasol, and silver bells. On the four sides of the base are shrines with gable-roofs.

芒达海寺塔　位于景洪市勐龙镇曼景列村。始建于清代中期，后多次修葺与重建。圆形台基，圆形须弥座，每层饰有仰莲，覆钟式塔身，塔刹由相轮、宝伞、银铃组成，通高约9米。塑有“妥纳妮”（司水的女神）等。

Mangdahai Vihara Pagoda is situated in Manlie Village, Menglong, Jinghong, and was built in the middle period of the Qing Dynasty. It has experienced some renovations throught its history. This 9-meter tall Stūpa has an overturned-bell-shaped body placed on a circular pedestal and Sumeru seat decorated with upturned lotus pedestal. The kshetra is composed of wheels, ornamental parasols and silver bells.

古吧罢阿念墓塔

位于景洪市勐龙镇曼景列村，芒达海佛寺内。始建于清代中期，后多次修葺与重建。塔为纪念清代勐龙著名佛爷古吧罢阿念而建，方形台基，折边“亚”字形须弥座，圆锥形塔身，塔刹由仰莲台、相轮、宝伞、银铃组成，通高约11米。

Gubaba Anian Grave Pagoda

Located in the Manlie Village, Menglong, Jinghong is the Gubaba Anian Grave Pagoda within the Mangdahai Temple, and it was built in the middle of the Qing Dynasty experienced several repairs in the history. The pagoda was so built to memorize a well-known Buddha locally around the Qing Dynasty in Menglong. The entire pagoda (11 m tall) was built on top of a square pedestal overlapped by a folded-edge X-shaped sumeru seat. Onward from the sumeru seat is a taper-shaped pagoda body connected to a kshetra composed of face-up lotus platform, wheels, treasure umbrella and silver bells.

曼龙叫塔　位于景洪市勐龙镇曼龙叫寨佛寺内。塔与寺始建于清代中期，后多次修葺、重建。方形台基，“亚”字形须弥座，塔身由方形三级“串”字形叠加而成，塔刹由相轮、宝伞、银铃组成，通高14.5米。塔基四角立佛龛座，仍保留着古朴端庄的原貌。

Manlongjiao Pagoda

Within the temple of Manlongjiao Village is a pagoda named simple after the village built in the middle Qing Dynasty through several repairs and reconstructions in the history. The entire pagoda (14.5 m tall) was built on top of a square pedestal overlapped by an X-shaped sumeru seat, while the pagoda body is finished in 3-graded gourd-shape connecting to a kshetra composed of wheels, treasure umbrella and silver bells. On the four corners of the pedestal are shrines.

曼纳塔　　位于景洪市勐龙镇芒栋村旁的山巅。傣语“塔庄朗”，意为山顶之塔。始建于清代中期，后多次修葺、重建。方形台基，折边“亚”字形须弥座，塔身为八边“串”字形，塔刹由多重相轮、宝伞、银铃组成。通高14.7米。台基四角立有方形塔式佛龛座。塔前是一条30多米的通道，两侧塑彩色巨龙守护。

Manna Pagoda is situated on top of a mountain adjacent to Mangdong Village, Menglong, Jinghong. It is also known as Tazhuanglang in Dai language, referring to a pagoda on the top of a mountain. It was built in the midst of the Qing Dynasty and has experienced some renovations in its the history. The octagonal gourd-shaped dome is placed on a square pedestal with multiple folds forming an X-shaped Sumeru seat. The kshetra is composed of multiple wheels, ornamental parasols and silver bells. The pagoda is totally about 14.7 m tall. The square tower-shaped shrines are set on the four corners of the base with a 30-m long pathway built in front of the pagoda, guarded by two giant colored dragons on both sides.

曼派舍利塔 位于景洪市勐龙镇曼派寨旁的山上。始建年代不详，多次修葺、重建。方形台基，塔身由多层折边“亚”字形须弥重叠而成，塔刹为石质，由多重相轮、宝鼎组成，呈圆锥形。塔身通高约7米，镶石碑。台基四角有莲花石雕佛龛座，全塔为金色。

Manpai Sarira Stūpa is situated on the mountain adjacent to Manpai Village, Menglong, Jinghong with an unknown date of construction, but it was renovated several times in the past. The dome is formed by multiple overlapping folds and an X-shaped Sumeru seat placed on a square pedestal. The entire golden pagoda is about 7m tall with a conical stone pagoda kshetra surmounted by multiple wheels and a peak of gems. A stone stele is inlaid in the stūpa and the sculptured stone lotus-shaped shrines are set at four corners.

曼宾塔 位于景洪市勐龙镇曼广罕寨旁。始建年代不详，后多次修葺、重建。为泰式金刚宝座式塔，由主塔和4座小塔组成。切角四边形台基，折边“亚”字形重叠须弥座，塔身呈圆锥形，塔刹由仰莲台与相轮、宝伞、银铃组成，通高约16米。小塔立于台基四角，开佛龛。全塔由几何图案和浮雕花纹装饰，金色为主色调。

Manbin Pagoda

Right beside Manguanghan Village Manlong Jinghong is the Manbin Pagoda with uncertain date of construction through several repairs and reconstructions in the history. This is a Thai-styled vajra pagoda (16 m tall) composed of one main pagoda and four baby pagodas all fixed to a cutting edged pedestal overlapped by an X-shaped sumeru seat with folded edge. The pagoda body was finished in taper shape connecting to a kshetra made up of a face-up lotus platform, wheels, treasure umbrella and silver bells. The four baby pagodas are erected all on the four corners with shrines. The entire pagoda is coated with golden color exquisitely decorated with geometric patterns and relief.

曼端佛塔　位于景洪市勐龙镇曼端寨旁，始建于清咸丰年间，后多次修葺、重修。塔基为方形，须弥座上是“串”字形与覆钟式组成的塔身，为八边形，塔刹由相轮、宝伞、银铃组成，通高约9米。台基四角设柱形仰莲小龛座。

Manduan Stupa

It is so named after the village nearby in Manglong, Jinghong built in the period of Xianfeng Reign of the Qing Dynasty experienced several repairs and reconstructions in the history. The entire pagoda (9 m tall) consists of a square pedestal overlapped by a sumeru seat, a gourd–shaped body finished on top with an over-turned bell. This octagonal pagoda is connected to a kshetra composed of wheels, umbrellas and silver bells. On the four corners of the pedestal are lotus-shaped shrines.

曼肯塔 位于勐龙镇曼肯寨塔园中。始建于民国初年，后多次修葺。群塔由主塔和6座小塔组成，主塔通高约17米，塔座为圆角方形，圆形须弥座，塔身呈圆锥形，塔的平面为八边形，塔刹由圆形仰莲台与相轮、宝伞、银铃组成。小塔与主塔形制相似，佛龛为双坡顶式，设于塔座四角。全塔装饰为金色。塔园护栏泥塑卧龙环绕，入口处一对白象迎客。

Manken Pagoda

Inside the garden of Manken Village, Menlong is the Manken Pagoda built in the beginning of the Republic of China. This golden colored octagonal pagoda consists of one main pagoda (17 m tall) and six baby pagodas all based on a round-corner disc and a round sumeru seat supporting a taper-shaped body. The kshetra is made up of a round face-up lotus platform, treasure umbrella and silver bells. All the four baby pagodas are built in the same constitution as that of the main pagoda. On the four corners are double-eave shrines.

曼秀塔　位于景洪市勐龙镇曼秀寨佛寺内。塔与寺始始建于清代，多次修葺、重修。塔座为方形，折边"亚"字形须弥座，塔身由"串"字形与覆钟式组成，为八边形，塔刹由仰莲台、相轮、宝伞、银铃组成，通高约11米。全塔为金色。

Manxiu Pagoda is situated in the Temple of Manxiu Village, Menglong, Jinghong. Both temple and pagoda were built during the Qing Dynasty experienced some renovations in the past. This golden pagoda is about 11m tall with an octagonal gourd-shaped body and an overturned-bell-shaped dome placed on a square pedestal with multiple folds and an X-shaped Sumeru seat. The kshetra is composed of an upturned lotus pedestal, wheels, an ornamental parasol and silver bells.

曼远塔　位于景洪市勐龙镇曼远寨佛寺内。塔与寺同建于清代中期，多次修葺。方形座基，折边“亚”字形双重须弥座，覆钟式塔身，塔刹由仰莲台和多重相轮、宝伞、银铃组成，通高10.4米。塔座与塔身饰有浮雕图案。塔为青灰色。

Manyuan Pagoda is situated in the Temple of Manyuan Village, Menglong, Jinghong. Both temple and pagoda were built during the Qing Dynasty. There have been some renovations in the past. On the square pedestal is an X-shaped overlapping Sumeru seat under an overturned-bell-shaped dome. The entire cinereous pagoda is about 10.4m tall with a kshetra composed of an upturned lotus pedestal, multi-wheels, an ornamental parasol and silver bells.

曼景列塔　位于景洪市勐龙镇曼景列寨佛寺内。塔与寺始建于清代中期，多次修葺。塔基与塔座为方形，六角形须弥座，塔身呈圆锥形，塔刹由多重相轮、宝伞、银铃等组成，通高12.4米。塔为金色。

Manjinglie Pagoda is situated in the Manjinglie Temple, Menglong, Jinghong. Both temple and pagoda were built during the Qing Dynasty. There have been some renovations in the past. On the square pedestal are a hexagonal Sumeru seat and a conical dome. The entire golden pagoda is about 12.4 m tall with a kshetra composed of multi-wheels, an ornamental parasol and silver bells.

曼归塔 位于景洪市勐龙镇曼归寨旁。始建年代不详，多次修葺。塔基为方形，高约1米，四围有护栏，垒石阶，立石雕灵兽守护。须弥座为折角八边“亚”字形。塔身为圆锥形。塔刹由多重相轮、宝伞、银铃等组成，通高约16 米。从须弥座到塔身都有花草、孔雀等浮雕图案装饰，塔为金色。

Mangui Pagoda is situated near Mangui Village, Menglong, Jinghong. The date of construction is uncertain, but it was renovated several times throughout history. This 16m tall golden stūpa was built on a one meter high square base with guardrails. The stone steps are guarded by stone-carved monster statues. The octagonal Sumeru seat was built into a conical X-shaped body with multiple folds. The kshetra is composed of multiple wheels, ornamental parasols and silver bells sculptured into flowers and peacocks in relief.

曼景罕佛塔 位于景洪市勐龙镇曼景罕寨佛寺内。塔与寺始建于清代末年，后重修扩建，佛寺规模宏大。佛塔为“亚”字形须弥座。塔身由“串”字形与覆钟式组成，塔的整体呈八边形，塔顶开四个小佛龛，内置圆雕佛像。塔刹由多重相轮、宝伞、银铃组成，通高约10米。塔为金色。

Manjinghan Pagoda is situated in the Temple of Manjinghan Village, Menglong, Jinghong. Both temple and pagoda were built in the end of the Qing Dynasty. There has been some large scale renovation and expansion in the past. On the X-shaped Sumeru seat, it is the gourd-shaped and overturned-bell-shaped dome, in octagonal form. The top of the pagoda is engraved with four small shrines for setting statues of Buddha. A golden 10m tall pagoda has a kshetra composed of multiple wheels, ornamental parasols and silver bells.

景尖佛塔　位于景洪市勐龙镇景尖寨佛寺内。寺与塔始建于清代中期，后多次修葺。群塔由主塔和4座小塔组成，主塔通高约16米。方形塔基围饰仰莲图案。须弥座底围饰大瓣仰莲，上为折边“亚”字形。塔身由八面体叠加“串”字形组成。塔刹由仰莲台和多重相轮、宝伞、银铃组成。小塔为方形，下开佛龛。塔基四围有雕塑卧龙守护。塔为金色，由花纹与浮雕图案装饰。

Jingjian Pagoda is situated in the Temple of Jingjian Village, Menglong, Jinghong. Both the temple and pagoda were built in the midst of Qing Dynasty. There have been some renovations in the past. The main pagoda is 16m tall, surrounded by four subsidiary pagodas engraved with shrines. On the square pedestal there is decorated a upturned lotus pattern. The Sumeru seat is surrounded by large petals of an upturned lotus and the tower has an X-shaped pattern which is covered by an octagonal gourd-shaped dome. The entire golden pagoda is engraved with relief associated with kshetra composed of an upturned lotus, multiple wheels, ornamental parasols and silver bells.

曼养广塔 位于景洪市勐龙镇曼养广寨旁。始建年代不详，多次修葺、重建。为泰式金刚宝座塔，由主塔和4座小塔组成。主塔通高约16米，须弥座为折角四方形，塔身由六角“串”字形与覆钟式组成，塔刹由多重相轮、宝伞、银铃组成。小塔分立四角，圆形塔身，塔刹与主塔相同。小塔下开双坡顶式佛龛，龛内置佛像。全塔由多层仰莲、缠枝浮雕图案装饰，为金色。

Manyangguang Pagoda is situated on the side of Manyangguang Village, Menglong, Jinghong. The date of construction is uncertain but it was successively renovated throughout its history. This golden, Thai-style, vajra-pagoda, decorated with multiple upturned lotuses and luxuriant relief of foliage is composed of the main pagoda and four small pagodas. The main pagoda is 16m tall with a folded square Sumeru seat and a hexagonal gourd-shaped dome. A pagoda kshetra is composed of multi-wheels, an ornamental parasol and silver bells. The small circular pagodas at four corners have separate shrines with gable roofs for setting statues of Buddha.

播勐龙塔 位于景洪市勐龙镇东风农场总部旁。始建于清初，后多次修葺。塔基呈八边形，周边饰有法轮和三角佛龛。塔座八边形，由12座雕塑精美的佛龛环绕组成须弥座。群塔由16座大小不一的小塔环绕主塔组成，塔身为圆锥形。塔刹由多重相轮、宝伞、银铃组成。主塔通高约23米，小塔通高约12～15米。群塔为空心砖塔，塔座下有4.5平方米，3米高的内室，塑多尊佛像。群塔的各个部位，用法轮、仰莲、动物、植物等多种图案装饰，气势恢宏，金碧辉煌，展示了傣族民间工艺的成就。

Bomenglong Pagoda is situated on the side of the headquarters of Dongfeng Farm, Menglong, Jinghong. It was built in the beginning of the Qing Dynasty and renovated several times afterwards. The conical dome with a Sumeru seat is surrounded by twelve exquisite shrines and is on the octagonal pedestal decorated with dharmachakra and triangle shrines. The pagoda group is formed by 16 conical pagodas of different sizes, and the hollow main pagoda is 23m while subsidiary pagodas range from 12 to 15m. The pagoda kshetra is composed of multiple wheels, ornamental parasols and silver bells. It has a small Buddha chapel covering an area of 4.5 square meters and is 3 meters in height under the base. All the pagodas are decorated with designs of dharmachakra, upturned lotuses, foliage and animals.

轰勐塔 位于景洪市勐龙镇帕扎寨旁的山巅。始建于清代中期，后多次修葺、重建。塔座为六边形，四角设双坡顶式佛龛座。须弥座为折边“亚”字形，四方置双坡顶式佛龛，内供佛像，龛门饰花纹浮雕。塔身由六面“串”字形与覆钟式组成。塔刹由多重相轮、宝伞、银铃组成。通高约19 米。八座佛龛的顶部均置塔刹。传说，此塔为镇伏北边补卧山的邪气而建，以保勐龙的兴旺。

Hongmeng Pagoda is located on the top of the mountain adjacent to Pazha Village, Menglong, Jinghong, and it was built during the Qing Dynasty and it has had renovations and reconstructions throughout its history. A 19-meter pagoda is sets up on a hexagonal base. It has gable-roof Buddha shrines with door frames carved in relief at the four corners. The pagoda kshetra is composed of multiple wheels, ornamental parasols and silver bells, which is set on the hexagonal gourd/overturned bell shaped dome. It has eight kshetra on the top of each shrine.

庄将塔　位于景洪市勐龙镇曼南块寨旁的山上，始建年代不详，多次修葺。塔基为方形，须弥座为折边“亚”字形，塔身由八面体“串”字形与覆钟式组成，塔刹由多重相轮、宝伞、银铃组成，通高约14米。台基四角立佛龛座，四围由雕塑卧龙连接佛龛座形成护栏，佛寺前有双面连体狮守护。塔为金色，有浮雕图案装饰。

With an uncertain date of construction and experienced several repairs in the history, the Zhuangjiang Pagoda is located on the top of the mountain adjacent to Nankuai Village, Menglong, Jinghong. On the square pedestal with shrines at the four corners and a folded edge X-shaped Sumeru seat, it is a 14m tall golden pagoda decorated in relief. It was built including the octagonal gourd-shaped and overturned-bell-shaped dome. The kshetra is composed of multiple wheels, ornamental parasols and silver bells.

勐龙中心塔　位于景洪市勐龙镇西南山巅上的佛寺内。始建于南宋嘉泰二年（1202年），历代多次修葺。傣名“塔布朗”，意为爷孙塔，相传为笃信佛教的爷孙俩倡建。因塔身为灰黑色，又称“黑塔”。塔基为两级折角四方形，边长约18米。群塔由主塔和4座小塔组成，须弥座为六方形阶梯式，塔身由“串”字形与覆钟式叠加而组成，塔刹由三层仰莲、覆莲、多重相轮、宝伞、银铃组成，通高17米，为金色。小塔立塔基四角，塔基、须弥座为方形，下开方形佛龛，塔身与塔刹与主塔相同。群塔与塔基用浮雕装饰，一级塔基四角有仰莲柱，四周有雕塑卧龙守护。为县级文物保护单位。

Menglong Central Pagoda, a cultural relic site under county-level protection, is located in the temple on the top of a mountain in the southwest of Menglong, Jinghong. It was built in the 2nd year of the Jiatai Reign of the Song Dynasty (A.D. 1202), and there have been renovations throughout its history. On the two-step folded angle square base, with a side length of 18 meters, the pagoda group with decoration in relief is composed of one 17-meter golden main tower and subsidiaries at the four corners with lotus columns. On the hexagonal Sumeru seat, with a retrogressive terrace and gourd-shaped overlapped, overturned-bell-shaped dome, it has a kshetra composed of a triple upturned lotus and an overturned lotus, multi-wheels, ornamental parasols and silver bells.

勐龙总佛寺塔　位于景洪市勐龙镇景弄寨总佛寺内（勐龙土司驻地总管宗教的佛寺）。寺与塔同建于明代中期，历代多次修葺、扩建。塔基为方形，双重须弥座为六边形，塔身由五层六边体叠加而成，塔刹由多重相轮、宝伞、银铃组成，通高约19米。全塔为金色，由多层仰莲与浮雕图案装饰，塔基四周设围栏。

The pagoda of Menglong General Temple is located in the General Temple, Jinghong Village, Menglong, Jinghong. Both the temple and pagoda were built during the Ming Dynasty with some renovations and expansions in the past. On the square pedestal and hexagonal Sumeru seat, decorated with lotuses and pattern in relief, it is a 19m tall golden pagoda, overlapped by five hexagonal bodies and a kshetra composed of multi-wheels, ornamental parasols and silver bells.

勐龙脚印塔 位于景洪市勐龙镇西南山巅的勐龙佛寺内。始建于明代中期，历代多次修葺。相传佛祖到此传经，留下足印，故建塔纪念。属泰式金刚宝座塔，由主塔和4 座小塔组成， 主塔通高9.7米。塔基为石砌正方形，空心须弥座为“亚”字形，开双坡顶式门，内藏佛足印。塔身由覆钵式叠加覆钟式组成，塔刹由多重相轮、宝伞、银铃组成。全塔雕刻多层仰莲图案。小塔分立须弥座四角，由覆钵式塔身和塔刹组成。

Menglong Footprint Pagoda, a Thai-style vajra-pagoda, including a 9.7m tall main pagoda and four small ones at four corners, is located in the Menglong Temple on the top of mountain in the southwest of Menglong, Jinghong. It was built during the Ming Dynasty, there have been some renovations in the past as a commemoration of Buddha's footprint. On the stone square pedestal and hollow X-shaped Sumeru seat is treasured foot print, the main pagoda is composed of overlapped, overturned-bell shaped and overturned-bowl shaped dome structures, while the small ones have an overturned-bowl shaped dome with multiple engraved upturned lotuses, and a kshetra composed of multi-wheels, ornamental parasols and silver bells.

万香勐塔　位于景洪市勐龙镇景乃寨佛寺内。塔与寺同建于清代中期，后多次修葺。寺内大殿、鼓房、僧房齐全，有彩绘佛经故事的壁画。群塔由主塔和 6座小塔环绕组成，主塔通高约16米，方形塔基，“亚”字形须弥座，塔身由“串”字形与覆钟式组成，塔刹由多重相轮、宝伞、银铃组成。塔基四角设方形佛龛座，塔为金色，有浮雕花纹装饰。

Wanxiangmeng Pagoda, a 16m main golden pagoda surrounded by six small ones with ornamentation in relief, is located in the Temple of Jingnai Village, Menglong, Jinghong. Both the temple and pagoda were built during the Qing Dynasty and there have been some renovations in the past. On a square pedestal with quadrangle shrines at the four corners, it is a pagoda including an X-shaped Sumeru seat, gourd-shaped and overturned-bell-shaped dome and kshetra composed of multi-wheels, ornamental parasols and silver bells.

嘎龙塔 位于景洪市勐龙镇嘎龙寨旁。始建年代不详，多次修葺。由主塔和4座小塔组成，主塔通高约12米，方形塔基，八角形塔座，塔身由“串”字形与覆钟式组成，塔刹由相轮、宝伞、银铃组成，小塔为方形，分立塔基四角。全塔为青灰色，仅饰有少许雕刻花纹与浮雕图案，风格古朴。

Galong Pagoda consists of one pagoda and four small ones at its four corners, is located on the side of Galong Village, Menglong, Jinghong. It is uncertain about the date of construction but it was renovated several times in its history. On a square pedestal with some ornamentation in relief, this is a 12m cinereous pagoda with the gourd shaped and overturned-bell shaped dome and the kshetra is composed of multi-wheels, ornamental parasols and silver bells.

庄勐塔　位于景洪市嘎洒镇曼占宰寨，始建年代不详，多次修葺。塔基为圆形，鼓形须弥座，“串”字形与覆钟式组成塔身，塔刹由莲瓣、多重相轮、宝伞、银铃组成，通高约14米，整体呈圆锥体。须弥座四方筑双坡顶式佛龛，龛顶设塔刹，佛龛之间塑雕圆柱形仰莲。全塔饰以金色和图案、浮雕。

The Zhuangmeng Pagoda is located on the side of Manzhan Village, Gasa, Jinghong. It is uncertain about the date of construction but it was renovated several times in its history. Built on the circular pedestal and drum-shaped Sumeru seat, it is a 14m golden pagoda decorated with pattern and relief, including gourd shaped and overturned-bell shaped dome, and the kshetra composed of multi-wheels, parasols and silver bells. On the four different directions of the Sumeru seat, the shrines with gable-roofs and pagoda-kshetra are set between columns with engraved upturned lotuses.

曼景保佛塔　　位于景洪市嘎洒镇曼景保寨佛寺内。寺与塔约建于清代末年，多次修葺。佛塔通高9.6米，方形塔基，方形“亚”字形须弥座，塔身由八面体“串”字形与覆钟式组成，塔刹由多重相轮、宝伞、银铃组成。塔座四周设围栏，入口处设一对小佛龛和一对雕塑灵兽。塔为金色，用浮雕图案装饰。

Manjingbao Pagoda is located on the side of Manjingbao Village, Gasa, Jinghong. Both the temple and pagoda were built in the end of the Qing Dynasty and there have been some renovations in the past. On the square pedestal and X-shaped Sumeru seat, a 9.6m golden pagoda with relief is formed by the octagonal gourd-shaped and overturned-bell-shaped dome, and the kshetra is composed of multi-wheels, ornamental parasols and silver bells. A guardrail is set around the pedestal and a pair of small shrines and animal statuettes line the way of entry.

庄兴塔　位于景洪市嘎洒镇曼养广寨佛寺内，始建年代不详，多次修葺。是著名的“九塔十二城”之一。塔通高约15米，方形塔基，六角形“亚”字形须弥座，覆钟式塔身，塔刹由多重相轮、宝伞、银铃组成。全塔呈金色，整体呈圆锥形，用浮雕图案装饰。

Zhuangxing Pagoda is located in the Temple of Manyangguang Village, Gasa, Jinghong. The date of construction is uncertain but it was renovated several times in its history. It is one of the famous "Nine Pagodas and 12 Towns." On the square pedestal and hexagonal X-shaped Sumeru seat, a 15m golden pagoda with relief is formed by the overturned-bell shaped dome, and the kshetra is composed of multi-wheels, ornamental parasols and silver bells.

班热塔　位于景洪市嘎洒镇景洪农场六分场卫生所对面的山上，是著名的“九塔十二城”之一。据资料载：此塔始建于傣历146年（784年），为唐代中期，多次修葺、重建。群塔由12座小塔环绕主塔组成。主塔通高约17米，方形台基，折边“亚”字形须弥座，塔身由八角“串”字形与覆钟式组成，塔刹由方形刹座、重叠相轮、宝伞组成。小塔与主塔形制相同，须弥座向外一面开佛龛。傣语“西双版纳”，意为十二块领地，每一座小塔象征着一块领地。主塔为白色，象征着圣洁。小塔为金色，象征着富饶。整座群塔极少装饰，仅主塔须弥座稍作变形处理。

Banre Pagoda consists of one white main pagoda and 12 golden small ones. It is located on the mountain opposite to the health center of the 6th branch of Jinghong Farm, Gasa, Jinghong. It was built during the Tang Dynasty (Dai calendar year 146 or A.D. 784) and has had renovations and reconstructions in the past. On a square pedestal, a 17m tall white pagoda is formed by the folded X-shaped Sumeru seat, octagonal gourd shaped and overturned-bell shaped dome and a square kshetra composed of overlapped-wheels and ornamental parasols. The small pagoda resembles the main one and has shrines set on the Sumeru seats.

庄莫塔 位于景洪市嘎洒镇猴山上，又称“庄莫塔”，是著名的“九塔十二城”之一。傣语“莫”为头骨，传说塔下埋着佛祖的头骨，每年赕塔活动十分隆重。今塔为明隆庆二年（1568年）所建。塔基为两层正方形，圆形须弥座，覆钟式塔身，塔刹由多重相轮、宝伞、银铃组成，通高10米。全塔为圆锥体，青灰色，有花纹与浮雕装饰。塔基四角有双坡顶式佛龛，正中较大的佛龛，内供佛像。为西双版纳州文物保护单位。

Zhuangmo Pagoda, a cultural relic site under protection of Xishuangbanna Prefecture, is located in the Monkey Mountain, Gasa, Jinghong, and was built at the 2nd year of Longqing Reign of the Ming Dynasty (A.D. 1568), as the legendary burial of Buddha's cranium. On the two-layered pedestal and circular Sumeru seat, it is a caesious conical 10m pagoda decorated with relief and floral ornamentation, including an overturned-bell shaped dome and kshetra composed of multi-wheels, ornamental parasols and silver bells. On the four sides of the pedestal are shrines for statues of Buddha with gable-roofs.

庄董塔　位于景洪市嘎洒镇猴山上，是著名的“九塔十二城”之一。始建于明代以中期，后多次修葺、重建。塔基为石砌两层正方形，有石阶。塔座为高身正方形，四面开双坡顶式假门佛龛。须弥座为三层圆形莲瓣台叠加。塔身为覆钟式。塔刹由多重相轮、宝伞、银铃组成，通高约14米。塔身由花纹、浮雕装饰，青灰色，端庄古朴，多处长出灌木类植物。

Zhuangdong Pagoda is located in the Monkey Mountain, Gasa, Jinghong, and was built during the Ming Dynasty. There have been some renovations and reconstructions in the past. Built on a stone square pedestal lined with steps and a cubic base with blank doors and gable-roofed shrines on four sides, it is a 14m tall cinereous pagoda decorated with floral relief, including a triple-lotus-petal Sumeru seat, overturned-bell-shaped dome and a kshetra composed of multi-wheels, ornamental parasols and silver bells.

曼端佛塔　位于勐海县勐海镇曼端村佛寺内。始建于清代中期，多次修葺。塔基为方形，侧面装饰浮雕、图案。须弥座为双重六边形，塔身呈“串”字形，塔刹由多重相轮、宝伞、银铃组成，通高14.4米。台基四角建双坡顶式佛龛，龛上置葫芦形塔刹。原塔为白色，重修时改为金色。

Manduan Pagoda is located in the Temple of Manduan Village, Menghai Township, Menghai County, and it was built during the Qing Dynasty and has been renovated several times afterwards. On the square pedestal, decorated with relief and patterns, and on double hexagonal Sumeru seat, is the 14.4m tall golden pagoda including a gourd shaped dome and kshetra composed of multi-wheels, ornamental parasols and silver bells. On the four sides of the base are shrines for statues of Buddha with gable-roofs and gourd-shaped kshetra.

曼端大白塔　位于勐海县勐海镇曼端村。始建于清初，多次修葺，后重建时扩大了规模与高度。群塔由28座小塔分立于四层不同高度的须弥座，层层上升，簇拥着主塔而组成，像一座高耸的山峰。折边“亚”字形塔基，塔身上部为覆钟式塔顶，塔刹由相轮、宝伞、银铃组成，通高约27米。塔基四角各建双坡顶式佛龛座，龛顶立与小塔相同的塔刹。须弥座上有相轮浮雕装饰。为仿泰国佛塔造型建筑。

Manduan Great White Pagoda is located in Manduan Village, Menghai Township, Menghai County, and it was built at the beginning of the Qing Dynasty. It has been renovated and expanded several times afterwards. As a modern imitation of a Thai pagoda, on the folded X-shaped pedestal, the 27m great pagoda stands among 28 baby pagodas on four-layered Sumeru seats with wheels in relief, including overturned-bell shaped domes and kshetra composed of wheels, ornamental parasols and silver bells. On the four sides of the base are shrines for statues of Buddha with gable-roofs and kshetra.

曼派佛塔 位于勐海县勐海镇曼派寨。始建年代不详，后多次修葺、重建。群塔由主塔和4座小塔组成，塔基为方形单层平台，须弥座为六角形，塔身为覆钟式，塔刹由相轮、宝伞、银铃组成，通高约12米。小塔分立塔基四角，开双坡顶式佛龛，高约9米，形制与主塔相同。群塔有浮雕、花纹装饰。

Manpai Pagoda is located in Manpai Village, Menghai Township, Menghai County. The date of construction is uncertain but it was renovated and reconstructed several times throughout its history. On a square single-layered pedestal, it is a 12m tall main pagoda, decorated with relief and floral patterns, including a hexagonal Sumeru seat, overturned-bell shaped dome and kshetra composed of wheels, ornamental parasols and silver bells. On the four corners of the pedestal are four small pagodas standing 9m tall with gable-roofed shrines for statues of Buddha.

曼路佛塔　位于勐海县勐海镇曼路村。始建于清代中期，后多次修葺。群塔由主塔和4座小塔组成。塔基为方形，高约2米，边长约8米。须弥座为折边“亚”字形。塔身为方形，分六级，每级四面开双坡顶式佛龛，第一级佛龛各供佛像一尊。塔刹由多重相轮、宝伞、银铃等组成，通高约13米。小塔立于塔基四角，须弥座与塔身为折边“亚”字形，形制与主塔不同。群塔为金色，有浮雕花纹装饰。

Manlu Pagoda is located in Manlu Village, Menghai Township, Menghai County, and it was built during the Qing Dynasty and renovated several times afterwards. Decorated by patterns in relief, it is a 13m main golden pagoda with folded X-shaped Sumeru seat surrounded by four small ones on a square pedestal, each one 2m in height and 8m in length. On the six-graded rectangular dome are gable-roofed shrines. On the four sides of the first level the statue of Buddha is placed. It is the kshetra composed of multi-wheels, ornamental parasols and silver bells. The lesser pagoda is composed of a folded X-shaped Sumeru seat and dome.

曼法金佛塔　位于勐海县勐海镇曼法寨旁的山上。始建年代不详，后多次修葺。方形塔基，须弥座为八边形上叠加折角亚字形，下层每边开佛龛，塔身由“串”字形和覆钟式组成，塔刹由多重相轮、宝伞、银铃组成，通高约13米。塔座四角立柱式仰莲，塔基四角立塔式佛龛座。塔座、塔身有部分浮雕纹饰。

Manfa Golden Pagoda is located on the mountain adjacent to Manfa Village, Menghai Township, Menghai County. The date of construction is uncertain, but it was renovated and reconstructed several times in its history. On the square pedestal and overlapped octagonal sections, it is a 13m tall pagoda with ornamentations in relief, including an X-shaped Sumeru seat with shrines and vertical upwards lotuses, gourd-shaped and overturned-bell-shaped domes, and the kshetra is composed of multi-wheels, ornamental parasols and silver bells. On the four sides of the pedestal are pagoda-style shrines.

曼来佛塔　位于勐海县勐海镇曼来佛寺内。寺与塔建于清代末年，后多次修葺。群塔由主塔和4座小塔组成，方形塔基与塔座。折边“亚”字形高基座，塔身第二层四面开佛龛。塔刹由多重相轮、宝伞、银铃组成。主塔通高约15米。小塔立于塔基四角，高约 6米，开佛龛。

Manlai Shūpa is located on the Temple of Manlai Village, Menghai Township, Menghai County. Both the temple and pagoda were built at the end of the Qing Dynasty and have had some renovations in the past. It is a 15m pagoda on square pedestal with folded X-shaped high-base dome that has shrines on the second layer. It is surrounded by four 6m small pagodas at its four corners with shrines. A kshetra is composed of multi-wheels, ornamental parasols and silver bells.

景恩塔　位于勐海县勐混镇城子村旁的广景恩山上。相传始建于唐代末期，历代多次修葺、重建，是勐混镇中心佛塔。群塔由主塔和8座小塔环绕组成，塔基为双层六边形，须弥座为六角折边“亚”字形，塔身由“串”字形与覆钟式组成，塔刹由多重相轮、宝伞、银铃组成，主塔高约20米。塔身满饰雕刻精细地蛟龙戏水、浮雕花纹等图案，全塔为金色。塔旁建有佛龛廊房，供朝拜用，为勐海县文物保护单位。

Jing'en Pagoda is a local central pagoda and a cultural relic site under protection in Menghai County. It is located on the Guang Jing'en Mountain adjacent to Chengzi Village, Menghai Township, Menghai County, and it is said to be built at the end of Tang Dynasty with some renovations and reconstructions in the past. A 20m tall main golden pagoda decorated with dragons in water and floral relief is encircled by eight small pagodas on a double-layered hexagonal pedestal. On a folded hexagonal X-shaped Sumeru seat, it is a gourd-shaped and overturned-bell-shaped dome, and the kshetra is composed of multi-wheels, ornamental parasols and silver bells. One shrine for worshiping Buddha with a Reignnda was built beside the pagoda.

曼章竜佛塔 傣语“塔瓦岗”，位于勐海县勐遮镇曼章竜寨佛寺内。始建于清代，后多次修葺，为泰式亭阁式塔。塔基为正方形，塔座为折边“亚”字形须弥座，塔身为三级折边“亚”字形须弥座和覆钟式塔顶组成，塔身一、二级每面开佛龛。塔刹由多重相轮、宝伞、银铃组成，通高约12米。塔座四角筑4座小塔，开佛龛。主塔以白色为主，塔顶饰金色，佛龛等部位饰金色浮雕花卉图案。

Manzhanglong Stupa

Within the temple of Manzhanglong Village Mangzhe, Manghai is this pagoda named after the village. It was built in the Qing Dynasty through several repairs. This is Dai-styled pavilion pagoda (12 m tall) based on a square pedestal overlapped by an X-shaped sumeru seat with folded edge. The pagoda has a 3-graded sumeru seat connecting to an overturned-bell top. On the first and second layers are opened with shrines on each side. The kshetra is composed of multi-layer wheels, treasure umbrella, and silver bells. On the corners of the pedestal are four baby pagodas with shrines built in. The main pagoda is mainly white except a golden decorated summit. In addition, the shrines and other spots are also decorated with golden color including relief and flowers.

勐混城子塔　位于勐海县勐混镇城子村。始建年代不详，多次修葺。塔座与束腰须弥座皆为八角形，“串”字形塔身，塔刹由圆形仰莲台与相轮、宝伞、银铃组成，通高约12米。须弥座四面设双坡顶式佛龛，上置小塔刹，塔身用浮雕仰莲、图案装饰。

Menghun Chengzi Pagoda

In the Chengzi Village of Menghun, Menghai is a pagoda (12 m tall) named after the place with uncertain date of construction through several repairs. Both the pedestal and the sumeru seat are built into octagonal shapes overlapped by a gourd-shaped body connecting to a kshetra made up of round face-up lotus platform, wheels, umbrella and silver bells. On the sumeru seat are double-eave shrines on four sides in associate with minor kshetra. The whole pagoda body is fitted with relief, lotus and flower patterns.

冬卖佛塔　位于勐海县勐遮镇曼么勒寨与曼方寨之间。塔与寺始建于清代初期，后多次修葺。群塔由主塔和8座小塔组成，塔基与塔座为圆形，主塔由“串”字形与覆钟形组成塔身，塔刹由多重相轮、宝伞、银铃组成，通高约17米。小塔形制与主塔相同，每座塔前设双坡顶式佛龛。全塔为金色。

Dongmai Pagoda is located between Manmele Village and Manfang Village, Mengzhe, Menghai. Both the temple and pagoda were built at the beginning of the Qing Dynasty with some renovations in the past. A 17m tall main golden pagoda is encircled by eight similar small ones, all having gable-roofed shrines separately on a circular pedestal and base. The main one contains a gourd-shaped and overturned-bell-shaped dome and a kshetra composed of multi-wheels, ornamental parasols and silver bells.

曼海竜塔　位于勐海县勐遮镇曼海竜佛寺内，傣语名“塔里丙斋”。塔与寺约建于明代末年，历代多次修葺。塔基为方形，四角建莲苞望柱，四边筑龙身围栏通石阶。塔座为方形，四面开双坡顶式佛龛。须弥座为折边“亚”字形。塔身由八边五级“串”字形与覆钟式组成。塔刹由多重相轮、宝伞、银铃组成。塔通高约17米。

Manhailong Pagoda is located in Manhailong Temple, Mengzhe, Menghai. Both the temple and pagoda were built at the end of the Ming Dynasty and have had some renovations in the past. On the square pedestal with lotuses and a stone guardrails with carved dragons, and on the square base with a gable-roofed shrine on four sides, a 17m pagoda is set including a folded X-shaped Sumeru seat, an octagonal five-graded gourd-shaped and overturned-bell-shaped dome and a kshetra composed of multi-wheels, ornamental parasols and silver bells.

贺允景叫塔　位于勐海县勐遮镇曼吕村委会三队，俗称“龟山大白塔”。相传始建于宋代（1028年），历代多次修葺、重建。塔基为方形砖砌有石阶、护栏的台座。须弥座为砖砌八面折边“亚”字形，每方置双坡顶式大佛龛，内供佛像。塔身由五级八面的“串”字形和覆钟式组成，第一级每边开4个双坡顶式小佛龛。塔刹由多重相轮、银铃组成，通高约27 米。塔基石阶两旁各彩塑一对卧龙守护，龙身蜿蜒于护栏，护栏外另立八座方形塔式佛龛。特点一，塔身与密檐式塔相似，塔顶部收分较小，融入了汉传佛塔的风格。特点二，佛龛数量之多极罕见，大小佛龛共计48个。

Heyun Jingjiao Pagoda is located in the jurisdiction of the 3rd team of the Manlu Village Committee, Mengzhe, Menghai, and it is said to have been built during the Song Dynasty (A.D. 1028) and has had some renovations and reconstructions in the past. On the square stone pedestal lined with steps and guardrails and the brick octagonal folded X-shaped Sumeru seat furnished with gable-roofed shrines, it is a 27m pagoda with in the Mahayana closed-eaves pagoda style. It includes an octagonal five-layered gourd-shaped and overturned-bell-shaped dome and a kshetra composed of multi-wheels and silver bells. Four shrines are built in every layer and eight shrines are outside the guardrail. There are a total of 48 shrines in all the pagodas.

景真中心塔　位于勐海县城西14公里景真山上，始建于南宋嘉泰四年（1205年），历代多次修葺、重建。方形台基上建有主塔和4座小塔，主塔通高约13米，折边“亚”字形高身须弥座，覆钟式塔身四方开双坡顶式佛龛，塔刹由仰莲座、相轮、宝伞、银铃组成。塔基四角筑小塔，形制与主塔相同，塔身皆为金色。为西双版纳傣族自治州文物保护单位。

Jingzhen Central Pagoda, a cultural relic site under protection of Xishuangbanna Prefecture, is located in the Jingzhen Mountain, east of Menghai, Jinghong, and was built in the 4th year of the Jiatai Reign of the Song Dynasty (A.D. 1205). There have been some renovations and reconstructions in the past. On the square pedestal with four small pagodas of same style built at the four corners, a 13m tall golden main pagoda was built on a folded X-shaped Sumeru high-base with overturned-bell-shaped dome made with four gable-roofed shrines and a kshetra composed of an upwards lotus, wheels, ornamental parasols and silver bells.

曼吕塔 傣语“塔瓦宰”，位于勐海县勐遮镇曼吕寨。始建于清代，后多次修葺。为泰式亭阁式塔，由主塔和4座小塔组成。塔基为正方形，四角设方形小塔，开佛龛。主塔通高约12米，须弥座为折边“亚”字形，塔身由三级方形折边叠加和覆钟式组成，每级每面都开佛龛，共12个，饰浮雕红底金花。塔刹由多重相轮、宝伞、银铃组成。塔身、须弥座为白色，五座塔顶饰金色。

Manlu Pagoda, a Dai-style pavilion-pagoda, is located in Manlu Village, Mengzhe, Menghai, and it was built during the Qing Dynasty. It has had some renovations in the past. On the square pedestal of four small pagodas with shrines at the four corners, it has a 12m tall main pagoda on a folded X-shaped Sumeru high-base with a three-layered overturned-bell-shaped dome. There are 12 gable-roofed shrines with relief and a kshetra composed of multi-wheels, ornamental parasols and silver bells.

西定佛塔　位于勐海县西定乡曼来寨旁的山上。始建年代不详，多次修葺。塔通高22米，塔基为正方形，折边亚字形须弥座，塔身呈圆锥形，塔刹由多重相轮、宝伞、银铃组成。须弥座下部四面设塔门式佛龛，内塑立式佛像，通道两旁塑波形卧龙。为近年新建。

Xiding Pagoda is located on the mountain adjacent to Manlai Village, Xiding, Menghai with an uncertain date of construction but it was renovated several times in the past. On the square pedestal, it is a 22m tall pagoda on a folded X-shaped Sumeru seat, with a conical dome and a kshetra composed of multi-wheels, ornamental parasols and silver bells. A blank-door shrine is set under the Sumeru seat for consecrating a standing statue of Buddha built recently.

勐遮总佛寺塔　位于勐海县勐遮镇召庄村勐遮总佛寺内。寺与塔始建于清代初期，佛寺规模宏大，由大殿、僧房、戒房、鼓房、佛塔组成。后多次修葺。群塔由主塔和4座小塔组成。塔基为方形，束腰折角亚字形须弥座，塔身为八边圆锥形与覆钟式组成，塔刹由多重相轮、宝伞、银铃组成，通高约12米。塔基上四角设佛龛座，外角立四座与主塔形制相同的小塔。群塔除塔基为白色，塔身皆为金色。

The pagoda of Mengzhe Gen Reignl Temple is located in the Mengzhe Gen Reignl Temple, Zhaozhuang Village Mengzhe, Menghai. Both temple and pagoda were built at the beginning of the Qing Dynasty. On the white square pedestal are niches of the statue of Buddha and four identical baby pagodas. A golden 12m pagoda was built including a girded and folded X-shaped Sumeru seat, octagonal conical and overturned-bell-shaped domes and a kshetra composed of multi-wheels, ornamental parasols and silver bells.

汪酷塔　位于勐海县勐遮镇曼老卖寨，始建于清代末年，后多次修葺。为泰式金刚宝座塔，由主塔和4座小塔组成。塔基为正方形，四角筑圆形佛龛座。塔座为八边形双层束腰须弥座，主塔由覆钵式与“串”字形组成塔身，四面设佛龛座，内供佛像，塔刹由多重相轮、宝伞、银铃组成，通高约14米。4座小塔环主塔而立，高约5米。塔身皆为白色，部分线条用金色装饰。

Wangku Pagoda is located in Manlaomai Village, Mengzhe, Menghai and it was built at the end of the Qing Dynasty. There have been some renovations afterwards. A white Thai-style vajra-pagoda decorated with golden lines is on a square pedestal with circular niches for Buddha statues surrounded by four 5m identical baby pagodas. A 14m tall main pagoda on an octagonal double-storied girded Sumeru seat is formed with overturned-bell-shaped and gourd-shaped bodies with shrines on all sides and a kshetra composed of multi-wheels, ornamental parasols and silver bells.

曼勐养塔　位于勐海县勐遮镇曼勐养寨佛寺内。寺与塔始建于清代中期，多次修葺。佛塔为泰式金刚宝座塔，由主塔和4座小塔组成。塔座为正方形，须弥座为正方折角“亚”字形，主塔塔身由“串”字形与覆钟式组成，一层塔身四面开佛龛，内供佛像，塔刹由多重相轮、宝伞、银铃等组成，通高约15米。塔座四角筑佛龛，上立方形小塔，形制与主塔相似。塔身皆为金色，用浮雕图案装饰。

Manmengyang Pagoda is located in the Temple of Manmengyang Village, Mengzhe, Menghai. Both temple and pagoda were built during the Qing Dynasty and have had some renovations afterwards. A golden Thai-style vajra-pagoda decorated with relief is composed of a main pagoda surrounded by corner shrines and 4 baby pagodas on square pedestal. On a square folded X-shaped Sumeru seat, a 15m main pagoda is set up, including gourd-shaped body with shrines on all sides of the first level as well as a kshetra composed of multi-wheels, ornamental parasols and silver bells.

瓦广塔　　位于勐海县勐遮镇曼章岭寨佛寺内，寺与塔始建于明代，历代多次修葺、重建。塔基为砖砌双重方形，四角筑塔式佛龛，内供佛像，须弥座为束腰折边“亚”字形，塔身由双重覆钟式叠加组成，塔刹由仰莲台、相轮、宝伞、银铃等组成，通高约13米。

佛寺大殿外壁彩绘《西塔》(释迦牟尼成佛故事)、《召苏塔努》等佛经故事。

Wanguang Pagoda is located in the temple of Manzhangling Village, Mengzhe, Menghai. Both temple and pagoda were built during the Ming Dynasty with some renovations and restorations afterwards. On the double brick-laying square pedestal with shrines at four corners, it is 13m tall pagoda composed of a girded folded X-shaped Sumeru seat and an overlapping kshetra composed of an upturned lotus, wheels, ornamental parasols and silver bells. On the wall of the temple is a painted Buddhist preaching of Xita (Buddha Sakyamuni's Life) and Zhaosutanu.

闸波塔　位于勐海县勐海镇曼拉闷寨旁的山丘上。始建于清代初期，后多次修葺、重建。傣语“塔闸波”，意为“莲花塔”。群塔由主塔和4座中塔、8座小塔组成。主塔通高约16米，塔座直径约5.6米，犹如巨钟倒扣。塔基与须弥座为圆形，须弥座四方开双坡顶式佛龛。塔身为覆钟式叠加方形宝瓶座组成，宝瓶座四方开佛龛。塔刹由相轮、宝伞、银铃组成。主塔为空心塔，东面设塔门，塔心内空2.5平方米，3米高，内供释迦牟尼佛塑像。12座中塔和小塔分立两台塔基上，皆开佛龛。群塔为金色，饰以法轮、仰莲、俯莲等浮雕图案。为近年仿缅式金塔而重建。

Naobo Pagoda is composed of one golden pagoda surrounded by four middle pagodas and eight baby pagodas on a two-layered pedestal. It is located on the hill beside Manlamen Village, Menghai, Menghai County and it was built at beginning of the Qing Dynasty with some renovations and restorations afterwards. The 16m main pagoda is on a circular pedestal with a diameter of 5.6m, and is composed of a circular Sumeru seat with rectangle gable-roofed shrines, overturned-bell-shaped overlapping, square Kundika dome with shrines and kshetra composed of wheels, ornamental parasols and silver bells. In a hollow main pagoda, it is an east pagoda shrine for the statue of Buddha Sakyamuni with an area of 2.5 m^2 , and 3m in height. It was recently restored in a style imitating the Myanmar golden pagoda decorated with Dharmachakra. It is decorated with an upward lotus and overturned lotus in relief.

宋杯塔　位于勐海县勐海镇曼喷竜寨。始建年代不详，清代以后多次修葺、重建。群塔由主塔和4座小塔组成。塔基为砖砌两台正方形，第一级四角筑塔式佛龛，第二级四角立和主塔形制相同的小塔。主塔通高18米，折边“亚”字形高基须弥座，塔身为叠加圆锥“串”字形与覆钟式组成，第一级四面设佛龛。塔刹由仰莲台、相轮、宝伞、银铃组成。群塔为金色，用浮雕仰莲装饰。

Songbei Pagoda includes a golden main pagoda and four baby pagodas. It is located in Manpenlong Village, Menghai, Menghai with an uncertain date of construction. There have been some renovations and restorations after the Qing Dynasty. On a square brick pedestal with shrines at the four corners of the 1st level and identical baby pagodas at four corners of the 2nd level, is an 18m main golden pagoda decorated with upward lotuses in relief, including a folded edge X-shaped Sumeru high base, conical pyramid with shrines on all sides and kshetra composed of upturned lotus, wheels, ornamental parasols and silver bells.

庄希里塔　位于勐海县勐海镇曼拉闷寨。始建于清代初期，后多次修葺、重建。塔基为砖砌两台正方形，四角置塔式佛龛。主塔通高约16米，须弥座为折边“亚”字形，塔身由须弥座往上变形为八角形、圆形、莲蕊式、宝瓶座。塔刹由仰莲台、多重相轮、宝伞、银铃组成。塔为金色，用浮雕仰莲花纹装饰。

Zhuangxili Pagoda is located in Manlamen Village, Menghai, Menghai and it was built at beginning of the Qing Dynasty with some renovations and restorations afterwards. On a two-stepped square bricklaying pedestal with shrines at four corners, it is a 16m main golden pagoda decorated with upward lotuses in relief and is composed of a folded X-shaped Sumeru seat, octagonal, circular, lotus-pistil-style, and Kundika-based domes, and kshetra composed of upturned lotus, multi-wheels, ornamental parasols, and silver bells.

勐海中心塔　位于勐海县勐海镇曼海寨旁的山顶。始建于清代初期，后多次修葺、重建。塔基为砖砌两层八角形平台，第一台置四座双坡式顶式佛龛和四只石雕灵兽，第二台每角置石雕莲蕊柱。须弥座为高腰折边“亚”字形，塔身由四级圆形仰莲台叠加和覆钟式组成，塔刹由仰莲台、多重相轮、宝伞、银铃、组成，通高约18米。塔为金色，饰以浮雕仰莲、花卉。

Menghai Central Pagoda is located on the top of the hill adjacent to Manhai Village, Menghai, Menghai and it was built at beginning of the Qing Dynasty with some renovations and restorations afterwards. On an octagonal double-layered bricklaying pedestal with four gable-roofed shrines and stone animals on the first level and stone lotus pillars on the 2nd level, it is a 18m golden pagoda with upward lotus and floral relief, including a folded edge X-shaped Sumeru high base, four-stepped circular upturned over-lapping lotuses with overturned-bell-shaped domes and kshetra composed of upturned lotus, multi-wheels, ornamental parasols and silver bells.

曼兴佛塔　位于勐海县勐海镇曼兴村旁山丘上的佛寺内。寺与塔始建于清代末年，多次修葺。塔基为砖砌两层正方形平台，四角置方形塔式佛龛。须弥座由折边“亚”字形重叠组成，塔身为覆钟式，塔刹由多重相轮、宝伞、银铃组成，通高约9米。塔为金色，仅用少量浮雕花纹装饰。

Manxing Pagoda is located in the temple on the hill in Manxing Village, Menghai, Menghai. Both temple and pagoda were built at the end of the Qing Dynasty with some renovations afterwards. On an octagonal double-layered bricklaying pedestal with square pagoda-like shrines at four corners, it is 9m tall golden pagoda with ornamentation in relief, including an overlapping folded-edge X-shaped Sumeru seat, overturned-bell-shaped dome and kshetra composed of multi-wheels, ornamental parasols and silver bells.

曼兴金塔 位于勐海县勐海镇曼兴村内。始建于清代中期，后多次修葺。塔基为砖砌方形平台，四角立方形塔式佛龛。塔座为六边形收分，须弥座为六角折边“亚”字形，塔身由圆“串”字形和覆钟式组成，塔刹由仰莲台、相轮、宝伞、银铃组成，通高约14米。塔为金色，极少装饰，古朴典雅。

Manxing Golden Pagoda is located in Manxing Village, Menghai, Menghai. It was built during the Qing Dynasty and there have been some renovations afterwards. On a square brick pedestal with square pagoda-shaped shrines at the four corners, it is a 14m tall golden pagoda with little decorations. It includes a hexagonal folded-edge X-shaped Sumeru seat, gourd-shaped and overturned-bell-shaped dome, and kshetra composed of upturned lotus, wheels, ornamental parasols and silver bells.

允香塔　位于勐海县勐海镇距曼兴村委会约1公里的山上。始建年代不详，后多次修葺。群塔由主塔和4座小塔组成。塔基为两层砖砌方形平台，第一层边长6米，四边正中置方形塔式佛龛。第二层边长5米，四角立小塔。主塔居小塔正中，通高约17米，上下收分甚小，须弥座为高腰折边“亚”字形，塔身由“串”字形体和覆钟组成，塔刹由仰莲台、多重相轮、宝伞、银铃组成。群塔仅用少许浮雕图案装饰，塔身修长俊秀，像一丛破土而出的金笋。

Yunxiang Pagoda consists of the main pagoda and four baby pagodas. It is located on the hill, 1km away from Manxing Village, Menghai, Menghai. It is uncertain about the date of construction but it was renovated several times throughout history. On a square double-layered brick pedestal with square pagoda-like shrines at the four corners of the 1st level and a side length of 6m as well as four baby pagodas on the 2nd level with a side length of 5m, it is a 17m central pagoda with relief, including a folded X-shaped Sumeru high base, gourd-shaped and overturned-bell-shaped domes and kshetra composed of upturned lotuses, multi-wheels, ornamental parasols and silver bells.

庄希里窝罕塔　位于勐海县勐阿镇曼派寨。始建于清代初期，后多次修葺。群塔由主塔和4座小塔组成，塔基边长约12米，为砖砌正方折边“亚”字形。主塔通高约16米，须弥座为八角折边“亚”字形，塔身由覆钵式和圆形“串”字形组成，底部四面开佛龛，内供佛像，塔刹由多重相轮、宝伞、银铃组成。小塔立于塔基四角，形制与主塔相同，下开佛龛。群塔除台基外为金色，饰以浮雕仰莲图案。

Zhuangxiliwohan Pagoda consists of a main pagoda and four baby pagodas at the four corners, it is located in Manpai Village,Meng'a, Menghai and it was built at the beginning of the Qing Dynasty. There have been some renovations afterwards. On a square X-shaped brick pedestal with a side length of 12m, it is a 16m golden main pagoda with upward lotus in relief, including an octagonal folded-edge X-shaped Sumeru seat, overturned-bell-shaped and circular gourd-shaped domes with shrines on all sides, and kshetra composed of multi-wheels, ornamental parasols and silver bells.

嘎赛金塔　　位于勐海县勐阿镇嘎赛村旁的山上。始建年代不详，历代多次修葺、重建。群塔由8座小塔环绕主塔组成，塔基为两层石砌圆形平台。主塔通高约18米，塔身由圆形“串”字形与覆钟式组成，塔刹由仰莲台、多重相轮、宝伞、银铃组成。8座小塔建于塔基上，通高约11米形制与主塔相同，前面开双坡顶式佛龛，内供8尊金佛。第一层塔基前，以佛龛、小塔、主塔为中轴线立石雕莲蕊佛龛。群塔为金色，各部位饰以精致地法轮、莲瓣、花卉、缠枝、灵兽、孔雀等浮雕图案。宝盖下的释迦牟尼金身坐像，通高6米有余，安详端庄，慈悲威仪。

Gasai Golden Pagoda consists of an 18m main pagoda and eight 11m baby pagodas and is located in the hill of Gasai Village,Meng'a, Menghai. It is uncertain as to the date of construction but it was renovated and restored several times in its history. On a stone double-layered circular pedestal, it is a golden main pagoda with circular gourd-shape and overturned-bell-shaped domes, and kshetra composed of upturned lotus, multi-wheels, ornamental parasols and silver bells. Eight gable-roofed shrines for golden statues of Buddha are built on the front of baby pagodas, and stone lotus pistil shrines are on the axis of the pagoda, set on a pedestal. It is decorated with various patterns, such as Dharmachakra, lotus-petals, florals, twigs, animals and peacocks in relief. A 6m sitting statue of Sakyamuni was built under a canopy.

曼迈塔　位于勐海县勐阿镇曼迈村2.5公里路旁的山巅上。始建于清代中期，后多次修葺、重建。塔基为砖砌方形两层平台，第二层塔基下筑方形塔式佛龛。塔座为四方高台折角须弥座，上层为圆型阶梯式叠加，塔身由三层仰莲台叠加和宝珠顶组成，塔刹由多重相轮、宝伞、银铃组成，塔身金色，通高16.5米。塔刹与塔身用刹杆连接，空心处可置灯。

Manmai Pagoda is located on the top of a hill, 2.5km away from Manmai Village, Meng'a, Menghaiand. It was built during the Qing Dynasty and there have been some renovations and restorations afterwards. On a square double-layered brick pedestal with square pagoda-like shrines at the four corners of the 2nd level, it is a 16.5m golden pagoda consisting of a square folded and circular Sumeru seat, a triple-upturned-lotus and pearl-like dome, and kshetra composed of multi-wheels, silver bells and ornate parasols.

款厚塔 位于勐海县勐阿镇曼本寨。始建于清代初期，历代多次修葺、重建。由主塔和4座小塔组成，塔基为石砌方形平台，四边正中垒石阶。须弥座为方形高台折边“亚”字形。塔身由覆钟式和“串”字形组成，四面开双坡顶式佛龛，内供佛像。塔刹由仰莲台、多重相轮、宝伞、银铃组成。通高18米，整体呈圆锥形。小塔建在塔基四角，方形塔座开佛龛，形制与主塔相似。除塔基外皆为金色，饰以多层浮雕仰莲、花卉等图案。

Kuanhou Pagoda consists of the main pagoda and four baby pagodas at the four corners with multi upward lotuses and flowers in relief. It is located in Manben Village, Meng'a, Menghai and it was built at the beginning of the Qing Dynasty. There have been some renovations and restorations afterwards. On a stone square pedestal with central steps, it is an 18m pagoda, including a square folded X-shaped Sumeru high base, overturned-bell-shaped and gourd-shaped domes with gable-roofed shrines for statues of Buddha on all sides, and kshetra composed of upturned lotuses, multi-wheels, ornamental parasols and silver bells.

机召香塔　位于勐海县勐阿镇曼波寨。傣语“机召香”，意为“一天建成”的塔。始建于清代初期，历代多次修葺。群塔由主塔和5座小塔组成，塔基为砖砌方形平台。主塔须弥座为方形折边“亚”字形，塔身由覆钵式与覆钟式重叠组成，塔刹较长，由仰莲台、多重相轮、宝伞、银铃组成，通高16.7米。主塔塔身的四面和与小塔的须弥座均开双坡顶式佛龛，主塔龛内供佛像。群塔饰以浮雕仰莲、花纹等图案，除青石塔基，为金色。

Jizhaoxiang Pagoda consists of the main pagoda and five baby pagodas decorated with upward lotuses and floral relief. It is located in Manbo Village, Meng'a, Menghai and it was built at beginning of the Qing Dynasty. There have been some renovations afterwards. On a brick square pedestal, it is a 16.7m main pagoda including a square folded X-shaped Sumeru seat, an overlapped overturned-bell-shaped dome, and kshetra composed of upturned lotus, multi-wheels, ornate parasols and silver bells. The gable-roofed shrines for statues of Buddha are built on all sides of the dome of the main pagoda and on the Sumeru seat of the turret.

曼松塔　　位于勐海县勐阿镇曼松寨旁的山上。始建于清代末年，多次修葺。群塔由主塔和4座中塔、4座小塔组成，方形塔基为两层石砌阶梯式平台，第一级塔基四角建小塔开佛龛。第二级塔基上叠加方形塔座，四角建中塔，中心建主塔，须弥座为六边高腰折边“亚”字形，塔身由“串”字形体与覆钟组成，塔刹由仰莲台、相轮、宝伞、银铃组成，通高14.8米。群塔形制相同，除台基外，塔身皆为金色，仅有少许浮雕莲花图案装饰。

Mansong Pagoda consists of a main pagoda, four middle pagodas and four baby pagodas decorated with little lotuses. It is located on the hill beside Mansong Village, Meng'a, Menghai and it was built at the end of the Qing Dynasty with some renovations afterwards. On a square double-layered stone pedestal with baby pagodas and shrines at four corners of the 1st level and a square base with middle pagodas on the 2nd level, it is a 14.8m central pagoda including hexagonal folded X-shaped Sumeru high base, gourd-shaped and overturned-bell-shaped domes and kshetra composed of upturned lotuses, wheels, ornate parasols and silver bells.

莲花白塔 位于勐海县勐阿镇后山顶上，始建年代不详，后多次修葺、重建。为泰式金刚宝座塔，由主塔和4座小塔组成。塔基为方形折边亚字形。主塔通高约16 米，须弥座为八边形宽底渐收两层仰莲座，第一层四面开券门佛龛，塔身由八角莲盆与圆柱体组成，塔刹由仰莲葫芦座、多重相轮、宝伞、银铃组成。群塔为白色，用金色描绘仰莲瓣、花草纹。

Lotus White Pagoda, a white Thai-style vajra-pagoda, including a main pagoda and four baby pagodas, is located on the mountain of Meng'a, Menghai with an uncertain date of construction but it was renovated and restored several times in its history. On a square folded-edge X-shaped pedestal, it is a 16m tall main pagoda on an octagonal double-upturned lotus Sumeru seat with arch shrines on all sides of the 1st level, and domes composed of upward lotus, gourd base, multi-wheels, ornate parasols and silver bells.

勐昂菩提塔　位于勐海县布朗族乡勐昂村佛寺旁。始建于清代末年，后多次修葺、重建。通高约11米，塔基为砖砌圆形平台，六角形塔座，圆形须弥座，覆钟式塔身，四面设佛龛，内供佛像。塔刹的第一层相轮体积特别大，与其覆钵式塔身的顶部直径相近，随即不断叠加的八级相轮急剧收分，占塔身高度的一半，上饰宝伞、银铃。塔的整体呈圆锥形，金色，局部饰以浮雕花纹图案。塔的四周塑有洗发的土地女神、司水女神“妥纳妮”和释迦牟尼佛像，还有白象、白马等。

Meng Ang Bodhi Pagoda, a conical pagoda with relief, is located in the temple of Meng'ang Village, Bulang Township, Menghai. It was built at the end of the Qing Dynasty and there have been some renovations and restorations afterwards. On a circular brick pedestal and hexagonal pedestal, an 11m golden pagoda on a circular Sumeru seat was built including an overturned-bell-shaped body, with shrines for statues of Buddha on all sides, and kshetra with overlapped gradually-decremented and overturned-bowl-shaped wheels, ornate parasols and silver bells.

南山梭塔　位于勐海县布朗族乡曼因村。始建年代不详，历代多次修葺、重建。塔基为两层砖砌八边形平台，塔座为八边莲瓣低台“亚”字形，须弥座为高台折边“亚”字形，塔身由三级莲盆“串”字形与覆钟式组成，塔刹由仰莲座、多重相轮、宝伞、银铃组成，通高约11米。塔基四角设双坡顶式佛龛座，塔身为金色，饰浮雕花纹图案。

Nanshansuo Pagoda is located in Mannan Village, Bulang Township, Menghai with an uncertain date of construction but it was renovated and restored several times throughout history. On a brick, double-layered octagonal pedestal and octagonal X-shaped low-terraced octagonal with a gable-roofed niche for Buddha's statue at the four corners. It is an 11m pagoda decorated in relief comprised of a folded X-shaped Sumeru high base, triple-graded-lotus-peviform gourd-shaped and overturned-bell-shaped body, and kshetra composed of multi-wheels, ornate parasols and silver bells.

曼班佛塔 位于勐海县布朗族乡曼班村。始建于清代中期，历代多次修葺、重建。塔座为八边莲瓣低台“亚”字形，须弥座为高台方形折角“亚”字形，塔身由三级莲盆“串”字形与覆钟式组成，塔刹由仰莲台、多重相轮、宝伞、银铃组成，通高15.7米。从塔基到塔顶全用浮雕仰莲、俯莲图案装饰，雕刻精致考究。

Manban Pagoda is decorated with upward lotuses and overturned lotus relief. It is located in Manban Village, Bulang Township, Menghai and it was built during the Qing Dynasty with some renovations and restorations afterwards. On an octagonal X-shaped low-terraced octagonal pedestal, a 15.7m pagoda was built on the square folded-edge X-shaped Sumeru high base with triple-graded lotus-flower-shaped bowl, gourd-shaped and overturned-bell-shaped body, and kshetra composed of upturned lotus, multi-wheels, ornate parasols and silver bells.

塔型建筑物

Pagoda-shaped Architectures

在云南的古代建筑中，有一种具有桥梁或古塔的外形，但又不具桥梁和古塔功能的建筑物，在建筑分类上造成了麻烦。例如邱北县的云南省文物保护单位，象鼻古水利工程，外表像一座桥，横跨在一条河上，而实际它是渡槽而不是桥，老百姓称它是“桥背水”；而在云南西双版纳州和德宏州，我们可以看到不少形状如塔而功能却是水井的建筑物，我们称它是塔还是井好呢？国家旅游局2003年出台的《旅游资源调查与评价》，帮我们解决了这道难题。我们可以把这类外形似塔而功能不是塔的建筑物，统称为“塔形建筑物”。

It is difficult to discern a kind of ancient architecture in Yunnan according to any existing category since they do not function as bridge or ancient pagoda but in the form of bridge or ancient pagoda. For instance, Xiangbi Ancient Irrigation Works, a bridge-shaped architecture across a river is actually an aqueduct. In reality, there is much architecture functioned with well in the form of pagoda in Xishuangbanna and Dehong, Yunnan. It is in a puzzle about the matter how to define this kind of architecture. In conformity with Investigation and Evaluation of Tourism Resource in 2003 by the State Tourism Administration, all those construction in the form of pagoda but without function of pagoda are collectively called Pagoda-shaped Architecture.

①②
③④

①地藏寺经幢
Kşitigarbha Temple Sutra Dhvaja (Banna)
②天乙庵石塔
Tianyi'Nunneny Stone Tow
③曼贺科井塔
Manheke Well Tower
④曼包宋井塔
Manbaosong Well Tower

①景宽寨井塔
Mankuan Village Well Tower
②曼哈总佛寺塔门
Manha Zongfo Temple Tower Gate
③曼法井塔
Manfa Well Tower
④漫洪井塔
Manhong Well Tower

①②
③④

①曼派寨心塔
Manpai Village Pagoda
②曼肯井塔
Manken Well Tower
③景乃大井塔
Grean Well Tower at Jingnai
④曼勐井塔
Manmeng Well Tower

①曼费井塔
Manfei Well Tower

②勐龙佛寺
Menglong Buddha-Stūpa

③曼康井塔
Mankang Well Tower

④曼董井塔
Mandong Well Tower

①②
③④

①曼秀井塔
Manxiu Well Tower
②曼养罕井塔
Manyanghan Well Tower
③龙曼掌井塔
Longmanzhang Well Tow
④中心井塔
Central Well Tower

①②
③④

①曼劳井塔
Manpang Well Tower
②帕扎井塔
Paza Well Tower
③曼缅井塔
Manmian Well Tower
④曼海竜井塔
Manhai Well Tower

①②
③④

①总佛寺门塔
Zongfo Temple Gate Pagoda

②总佛寺纪念塔
Zongfo Temple Cenotaph

③曼景保井塔
Manjingbao Well Tower

④爹长龙水井塔
Diechanglong Well Tower

①②
③④

①曼路井塔
Manlu Well Tower
②曼端井塔
Manduan Well Tower
③景真亭塔
Jingzhen Pavilion Tower
④召庄寺塔
Zhaozhuang Temple Pagoda

① ②
③ ④

①景乃井塔
Jingnai Well Tower
②曼洪么井塔
Jinghongme Well Tower
③嘎洒藏经塔
Gasa Tibetan Sutra Pagoda
④曼栋井塔
Mandong Well Tower

参考文献：

1.《云南名胜古迹辞典》，邱宣充主编，云南科技出版社出版1999年1月第1版。
2.《云南省志.宗教志》，云南省社会科学院宗教研究所编撰，云南人民出版社出版1995年9月第1版。
3.《中国塔》，张驭寰著，山西人民出版社出版2000年12月第1版。
4.《擎天摩云的七宝庄严———古代名塔》，罗哲文著，辽宁师范大学出版社出版1996年10月第1版。
5.《中国古塔》，夏志峰 张斌远著，浙江人民出版社出版 1996年10月第1版。
6.《中国塔林漫步》，徐伯安著，中国展望出版社出版 1988年7月第1版。
7.《中国古塔造型》，徐华铛著，中国林业出版社出版 2007年6月第1版。
8.《西双版纳佛塔的类型及其源流》，作者 罗廷振，南京博物院：《东南文化》1994年6期。
9.《傣族佛塔漫谈》，作者 索南才让，今日民族杂志社：《今日民族》2008年 6期。
10.《云南地名之奥秘》，吴光范著，德宏民族出版社出版1993年5月第1版。
11.《大理白族自治州志》(卷七)，云南人民出版社出版2000年11月第1版。
12.《保山地区志》，中华书局出版1998年3月第1版。
13.《思茅地区志》，云南民族出版社1996年10月第1版。
14.《巍山彝族回族自治县志》，云南人民出版社出版1993年12月第1版。
15.《景洪县志》，云南人民出版社出版2000年6月第1版。
16.《勐海县志》，云南人民出版社出版1997年12月第1版。
17.《勐腊县志》，云南人民出版社出版1994年2月第1版。
18.《临沧县志》，云南人民出版社出版1993年12月第1版。
19.《禄丰县志》，云南人民出版社出版1997年12月第1版。
20.《大关县志》，云南人民出版社出版1998年12月第1版。
21.《剑川县志》，云南民族出版社出版1999年12月第1版。
22.《洱源县志》，云南人民出版社出版1996年12月第1版。
23.《祥云县志》，中华书局出版1996年3月第1版。
24.《新 西双版纳风物志》，征鹏 杨胜能 编著，云南人民出版社出版1999年4月第1版。
25.《新 德宏风物志》，张方元 主编，云南人民出版社出版2000年5月第1版。
26.《新 思茅风物志》，黄桂枢 编著，云南人民出版社出版2000年5月第1版。
27.《新 临沧风物志》，武定云 编著，云南人民出版社出版2000年8月第1版。

References

1. Dictionary of Yunnan's Famous and Historical Sites Chief Editor Qiu Xuanchong
2. Yunnan Provincial Chorography. Religious Chorography Edited and writteny Religiuos Research Institute of Yunnan Provincial Academy of Social Sciences
3. Chinese Pagodas By Zhang Yihuan
4. Famous Ancient Pagodas, the Seven Grandeur Pagodas Towering to the Sky By Luo Zewen
5. Chinese Ancient Pagodas By Xia Zhifeng
6. Some Thoughts on Chinese Forest of Pagodas By Xu Bo'an
7. Sculpts of Chinese Ancient Pagodas By Xu Huadang
8. Categories of Pagodas in Xishuangbanna and their Origins and Developments By Luo Yingzhen
9. Pondering over Stupas Worshipped by Dai Ethnic Group Written by Suonan Cairang
10. Arcanum of Toponym in Yunnan By Wu Guangfan
11. Chorography of Dali Bai Autonomous Prefecture Vol. VII
12. Chorography of Baoshan Region
13. Chorography of Simao Region
14. Chorography of Weishan Yi and Hui Autonomous County
15. Chorography of Jinghong County
16. Chorography of Menghai County
17. Chorography of Mengla County
18. Chorography of Lincang County
19. Chorography of Lufeng County
20. Chorography of Daguan County
21. Chorography of Jianchuan County
22. Chorography of Er'yuan County
23. Chorography of Xiangyun County
24. Records of Scenery in Xishuangbanna (Updated) By Zheng Peng, Yang Shengneng
25. Records of Scenery in Dehong (Updated) Edited by Zhang Fangyuan
26. Records of Scenery in Simao (Updated) Edited by Huang Guishu
27. Records of Scenery in Lincng (Updated) Edited by Wu Dingyun

后记

邱宣充

我很有幸，早在上世纪六十年代就跟随马曜先生在西双版纳调查南传上座部佛教和原始宗教，我所调查的主要内容是景洪的佛教建筑。上世纪八十年代，我又参加了维修大理崇圣寺三塔，从事文物考古发掘和勘测工作。退休之后在本世纪初又有机会参加祥云水目山北岗塔林的维修，近年又进行盈江允燕塔保护规划的指定工作，从此和云南的古塔结下了不解之缘。

同时我很钦佩本书的两位作者陈云峰和张俊先生。因为拍摄古塔很不容易，他们跑偏了全省各地，由于古塔大多建在山顶之上，而且塔体高耸，取一个全景，找一个好的视角，均要付出艰辛的劳动。

古塔建筑是中华古代文明的组成部分，是建筑文化的精粹，云南古塔更是云南多元文化的象征。

首先密檐式方塔是我国中原地区唐代古塔的一种基本造型，而云南古塔亦是以密檐方塔为基本造型，而且延续千年之久，这种文化的渊源关系十分清晰。同时，古代文化的传承往往存在这样的现象：即在一种文化发源的地方已经消失的东西，却在它的传承地完整地保存着，这在一些边远省份反映十分明显。例如唐代武则天统治时期通行一种改创文字（如“国”字写成“圀”字），在中原早已弃用，然而在云南则一直沿用至大理国时期；又如明王朝在云南实行军屯，大批汉族居民迁居云南，当时明代妇女流行的服装服饰，至今仍可在云南农村老年妇女服装中找到它的痕迹。而密檐方塔虽然唐代中原地区盛极一时，但唐代以后，除洛阳的白马寺塔（金）、河南密县的法海寺塔（宋）、武安县灵泉寺塔（宋）、辽宁朝阳的凤凰山塔外，其余均由八角形楼阁式塔所代替，而云南的密檐方塔历唐、宋、元、明、清各代经久不衰，并由佛教领域扩展到道教和儒教的建筑领域之中，在全国来说可以说是集密檐方塔建筑艺术之大成。

云南地处祖国西南边疆，有三千余公里的国境线与缅甸、泰国、越南、老挝等东南亚国家相邻，由于边境民族地区民众信仰南传上座部佛教，在佛教建筑文化领域中吸收东南亚地区文化的影响是十分自然和明显的事。这种文化交融也有上千年的历史，缅甸式的、泰国式的、印度式的佛塔建筑同时出现在我国的领土上，构成云南古塔建筑另一个鲜明的地方特色，然而云南的民族建筑绝不是一味照搬外来的建筑文化，而是与当地的民族文化相融合，这种文化交流和相融的现象，改革开放以来还有进一步加速的趋势。例如本书收录西双版纳某几座形体高大而明显用钢筋水泥建筑而成的佛塔，严格来讲不属于古塔，但为了全面反映建筑艺术的发展趋向和反映佛塔建筑多元文化因素的客观存在，我们依然收录在本书之中。我们认真研究和总结这种文化现象，对于探讨边疆民族建筑文化的发展无疑是一件有意义的事。

2008年12月于昆明

Postscript

Qiu Xuanchong

Ancient pagodas are significant cultural heritage sites in Chinese architectural history. They form an integral part of the multi-disciplinary cultures of Yunnan.

Dense-eave square pagodas were popular forms of the ancient pagodas found in Yunnan; they first originated in central China, occupying a predominant place amongst the ancient pagodas of the Tang Dynasty. Even after many centuries, it was still possible to distinguish their cultural influence.

Furthermore, due to its geographical distance from the mainland, Yunnan fortunately has prolonged the life span of these ancient pagodas, while in many places in China, traces of this cultural expression have long since died out.

During the reign of Wuzetian in the Tang Dynasty, a revolution of Chinese characters was implemented throughout China. Later, this cultural reform was successfully continued until the time of the Dali Kingdom while it was abandoned in the mainland provinces. Another cultural trace originating in central China and later found in Yunnan includes a military station erected during the Ming Dynasty, during a time when a great number of Han people moved to Yunnan. Thus, the fashionable costumes of the Tang Dynasty are frequently seen amongst the rural senior ladies of Yunnan.

In old China, especially during the Tang Dynasty, dense-eave square pagodas were in fashion for a period of time, in particular around the central plains. Nowadays, most pagodas in the central plains are octagonal pagodas instead of dense-eave ones, except for the White-Horse Temple Pagoda (built in the Jin Dynasty) in Luoyang, the Fahai Temple Pagoda in Mixian (built in the Song Dynasty), the Lingquan Temple Pagoda in Wu'an, and the Phoenix Mountain Pagoda in Chaoyang, Liaoning.

The dense-eave square pagodas have recorded innumerable historical events throughout the centuries, from the Tang Dynasty forwards. The building of dense-eave square pagodas was expanded from originally being only a manifestation of Buddhism to Taoism and Confucianism as well. They provide architectural historians of China with hard-to-get art relating to this form of ancient pagoda.

Yunnan, owing to its distinctive location on the southwest border of China, ranges over 3,000 km of national boundary line, sharing similar cultural experiences with neighboring countries, such as Vietnam, Thailand, Myanmar, Laos and the nearby Southeast Asian countries. Obviously, we can often detect the interlinked connections between Yunnan and its neighboring countries resulting from the shared beliefs of Southern Buddhism. To conclude, the ancient pagodas of Yunnan constitute important cultural relics in our country, mingling with histories covering thousands of years. They also function as an epitome of cultural exchange with neighboring countries, represented by Burmese style pagodas, Thai-style pagodas and Indian stūpas.

Such cultural combinations between different ethnic groups are now further accelerated after the opening and reform of China. Clearly, some large-scaled Buddha-stūpas in Xishuangbanna described in this album were built with reinforced bars and cement, and do not at all comply with the specification as ancient pagodas. They can only be seen as examples of cultural development trends over the course of history. We insist on including them in our analysis, as we definitely believe they play an important role in the study of ethnic architecture in Yunnan.

Kunming
December 2008

图书在版编目（CIP）数据

云南古塔建筑/陈云峰，张俊编著.—昆明：云南美术出版社，2008.12
ISBN 978-7-80695-797-4

I.云… II.①陈…②张… III.塔—古建筑—简介—云南省 IV.K928.75

中国版本图书馆CIP数据核字（2008）第207770号

策　　划：彭　晓　张晓源
英文翻译：云南新宇翻译有限公司
英文校审：Mitchell Kelner, Timothy De Lise
英文审校：康文梅
校　　对：董　明
中文审校：方绍忠
整体设计：庞　宇
绘　　图：宇广龙
责任编辑：张晓源　庞　宇

雲南古塔建築（下）

Yunnan Ancient Pagodas (Vol.2)

摄　　影：陈云峰
撰　　文：张　俊
出版发行：云南出版集团公司
　　　　　云南美术出版社
制　　版：昆明雅昌图文信息技术有限公司
印　　刷：昆明富新春彩色印务有限公司
开　　本：890×1230mm 1/20
印　　张：15.2
版　　次：2008年12月第1版
　　　　　2008年12月第1次印刷
印　　数：1-4000
ISBN 978-7-80695-797-4
定　　价：160.00元（上下）